CELTIC
KNOTWORK
DESIGNS

CELTIC
KNOTWORK
DESIGNS

Sheila Sturrock

GUILD OF MASTER CRAFTSMAN PUBLICATIONS LTD

First published 1997 by
Guild of Master Craftsman Publications Ltd,
166 High St, Lewes,
East Sussex BN7 1XU

ISBN 1 86108 040 9

The publishers would like to thank: the Manchester Metropolitan
University for their kind permission to reproduce the Eternal Knot
and Celtic Cross designs on pages 6 and 7, both from the
Laura Seddon Collection; and Robin Dengate for his kind permission
to reproduce his photo, Well Dressing, on page 35.

Photography for Chapter 21 by Dennis Bunn 1997

Illustrations by Guild of Master Craftsman
Publications Design Studio 1997

Designed by Guild of Master Craftsman Publications Design Studio
Typefaces: Cantoria, Sabon and Omnia
Colour separation by Global Colour (Malaysia)
Printed in Hong Kong by H&Y Printing Ltd

CONTENTS

Acknowledgements

It would be impossible to produce a book of this type without the assistance of people willing to test the designs. A very special thankyou must go to Carole Harrison, Read Primary School, who kindly 'lent' me her class to teach, and to Jack Dowling, Smallbridge Primary School, Rochdale, who passed on his enthusiasm to his own class with outstanding results. Thankyou to Val Fynan and the East Lancashire Calligraphy Group for their encouragement and support. Also to the following people who so generously gave their time to work examples and to write about their crafts: Margaret Bolton, Carrickmacross lace; Maureen Bowe, patchwork; Val Fynan, embossed cards; Norma Gregory, pokerwork; Kate Haines, cross stitch, beading, Assisi work and embroidery; Mary Heap, calligraphy; Marion Holden, china painting; Bonnie Kramrisch, parchment craft; Karen Quickfall, needlelace; Susan Lord, quilling; Pauline Stone, bobbin lace; Henry Sturrock, wood carving; John Sturrock, knitting; Moray Sturrock, squared charts; Stephanie Sturrock, free design; Hayley Clancy (9) for permission to include her dalmation knot; and Ruth Pogson for her assistance with the coloured knotwork examples.

INTRODUCTION

T his book has been written for all those people who have tried plotting Celtic knotwork but have, as yet, failed, and for all craft workers who wish to use Celtic knotwork in their designs. There are books of ready-made designs which are excellent, but these do not teach the essential element of construction which enables students to combine designs and adapt them to their own requirements, as did the ancient scribes.

I developed my method of construction out of frustration, and quite by chance. Having failed to follow other methods I drew hearts, which are a common design feature, over a sheet of paper and joined them by extending diagonal lines from their centres. This produced a knotwork design, and I found that by varying the placement of hearts and joining lines, different designs were produced. I then moved on to starting with larger hearts, which gave me the space for more interweaving, then modified the hearts by extending the base and the top. Each change in the basic heart led to different designs and different effects.

By breaking knotwork down into a series of curves and lines, plotting all the curves on squared graph paper, and then joining them together with lines, the construction became simple, with no need for complicated measurements and counting. Curves and lines make up the two basic units of all designs plotted using this technique - hearts and loops - so anyone who can draw a simple heart and interweave correctly will have no difficulty in executing what appear to be very complicated patterns.

I have divided the book into chapters according to the basic construction unit of the designs, for example, all the patterns in Chapter 3 are constructed by first plotting a series of small hearts. Examples in each chapter demonstrate the different effects that can be produced through various ways of plotting curves and lines.

All the patterns illustrated are based on angles of 45°, 90°, and 180°, where traditional designs are much more flexible. The ancient scribes simply extended lines or pointed loops to fill irregular shapes. Once the basic principle in each chapter has been understood, you can experiment with plotting shapes in different positions, and move away from rigid plottings, adapting patterns to suit any size or shape required. Similarly, once the idea of zoomorphics (animal forms) becomes familiar, any animal, plant or man can be fashioned out of a convenient curve.

The designs illustrated are plotted on a grid of dots rather than on a graph to prevent possible confusion from too many lines. In each chapter designs are presented according to the number of squares required for a test design (a single draft of the complete design), commencing with the least number of squares across and down and gradually increasing in width and depth. This enables the reader to mark out an accurate grid for the test piece, and to select a design to fit the space available for decoration. The ordering is *not* according to difficulty. A design which uses a small number of squares is not necessarily less complex than a design which uses a large number. A square can be any size, so a design which requires eight squares across and five down is equally suited to a space of 8 x 5in (marked in 1in squares) or 40 x 25mm (marked in 5mm squares). What is important is that the space can be divided into the number of squares required to fit the particular design. Plotting exact graphs becomes less important as confidence is gained, and designs can be drawn over a few lightly pencilled dots.

PART ONE

Tools &
Techniques

Chapter 1

HISTORY

The Celts

During the seventh century BC, Celts arriving from the Continent began to settle in Britain. Celtic kings were often patrons of the arts, and the Celts are still known for their art, fine ornaments and jewellery. Their knotwork and interlacing patterns in particular are instantly recognized.

Knotwork was both a decorative and a religious art, borne from the oral traditions of the Celtic people and the beliefs they learned from the Druids. Celtic art had three main functions:

- depiction of stories;
- decoration; and
- religious symbolism.

According to Celtic beliefs, there are seven created life forms – plant, insect, fish, reptile, bird, mammal and man. These are all represented in Celtic art, but in a stylized and highly imaginative form, as to copy the art of the creator was forbidden. Human figures (anthropomorphics) depict men with interlaced limbs and extended beards, and animal forms (zoomorphics) are shown with extended and interweaving ears, tails and tongues.

Plaitwork and knotwork designs

Knotwork is developed from plaitwork. Plaitwork patterns consist of straight, diagonal lines joined together with curves, as in the example shown in Fig 1.1. They were used extensively in Roman, Greek and Egyptian art. (There are many patterns in Chapter 12, Straight Lines, which show how plaitwork can be developed into knotwork.)

In the sixth century AD, plaitwork was used extensively in Italian churches to decorate altar screens and covers for

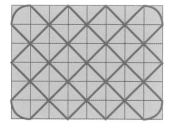

FIG 1.1 Roman plaitwork.

various church vessels. The plaitwork decorations of this time show a development from the early designs that opened up greater possibilities for the creation of more intricate patterns. Instead of using continuous diagonal lines, they used broken lines, which enabled interweaving.

The Celts also used broken lines in their own distinctive, interwoven knotwork (see Fig 1.2). Because they used their knotwork to decorate irregular spaces on stone crosses, manuscripts, jewellery and wood, they also added angular lines and pointed loops to fill in corners, and used a variety of motifs to close off knotwork ribbons. In this way, even the simplest ribbon could be woven into intricate patterns producing secondary ribbons, which were sometimes highlighted by using a different colour for each lacing.

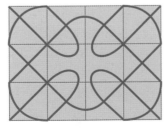

FIG 1.2 Celtic knotwork showing the break in lines in the centre.

Spirals and key patterns are also characteristic of Celtic knotwork design (see Figs 1.3 and 1.4). Spirals were the earliest motifs used in Celtic Christian art. They are patterns composed of circles (the circle being the symbol of perfection) which are joined together with shallow, elongated S- or C-shaped curves. Key patterns resemble the

FIG 1.3 Spiral patterns are common in knotwork designs.

notches of a key, the most recognizable of these being the Greek key pattern which appears to be a 'square' spiral, but is, in fact, a series of short horizontal and vertical lines. Celtic key patterns

FIG 1.4 A typical key pattern.

differ from this in that they also incorporate diagonal lines in the designs. All key patterns are made up of straight lines.

Materials

The designs were created using simple materials. Fine lines were drawn with the quill of a goose or crow feather, both of which could be fashioned to give a square end with a very fine point, and the designs were then scored using a

FIG 1.5 Example of an eternal knot design. These were very popular at the start of the nineteenth century.

stylus made from wood, iron or bone. (It is possible that silver points were also used.) Vellum was used for manuscripts. The difficulties of writing on a hairy surface such as this were overcome by the fineness and shape of the quill point. Writing on a hairy surface is rather like drawing with pen on a pile carpet. The square end of the quill allowed it to travel down through the vellum pile which enabled the scribe to draw on the actual skin rather than on the fine fibres.

With the design plotted, further details were superimposed in light coloured ink. Colour was applied to the edges with a quill, and large areas were coloured using a brush. Designs were sometimes highlighted by leaving small areas of the work unpainted.

Colours

Celtic artists had an astonishing knowledge of the chemical properties of pigments and their manuscripts were alive with vibrant colour. Many pigments were obtained from local sources: red from red lead; yellow (orpiment) from soil found in parts of Ireland; emerald green from copper; violet blue from the woad plant (also known as 'dyer's weed'); whites from white lead and chalk; and verdigris, a greenish-blue (a patina formed on copper, brass or bronze). Other pigments were imported: mauves, maroons and purples are thought to have been obtained from the Mediterranean plant *Crozophora tinctoria*; kermes (crimson) was produced from the pregnant bodies of insects *(Kermococcus vermilio)* that lived in the evergreen trees of the Mediterranean; and ultramarine, a rare and valuable pigment of brilliant blue, thought to have been obtained by crushing lapis lazuli, which was imported from the foothills of the Himalayas in north-east Afghanistan. Indigo, an oriental plant, was the source of a deeper blue.

FIG **1.6** Celtic cross decorated with a celtic knotwork design.

Chapter 2

Materials & Techniques

---◆---

MATERIALS

The materials required for Celtic knot-work are few and inexpensive.

Plotting

Graph paper is essential. I recommend 5mm squares as a convenient size for trying out most patterns and 1cm squares for complicated designs where a number of lines interweave, as a larger drawing makes it much easier to see each crossing point. Once the interweaving has been understood the actual work can be done on any size square.

Grids can easily be transferred from graph paper to plain paper by securing a plain sheet over a graph with masking tape, and using the graph squares to draw a grid on the plain sheet (see Fig 2.1).

A 2B pencil is best for plotting the designs as the lines produced are clear and the soft lead can be rubbed out easily once the design has been inked in. An 0.5mm automatic pencil is invaluable for this work. An automatic pencil allows a continuous supply of lead which does not vary in thickness and does not require constant sharpening as does a normal pencil. The 0.5mm lead combines strength with accuracy – the

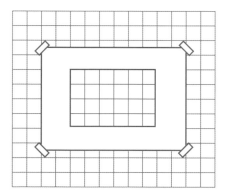

FIG 2.1 Attach plain paper to a background piece of squared paper with masking tape, and use the squares to draw a grid in the required position.

finer 0.3mm breaks too easily while the 0.7mm does not give the fineness and accuracy required.

Colouring

Water-soluble pencils have a waxy texture and give a good depth of colour which is easily controlled. After the design has been coloured in, water can be painted over the pencil marks to give the effect of a water-colour design – subtle shading can be introduced in this way. Felt-tip pens can be used to give an interesting shaded effect to ribbonwork, especially in large designs where the colour 'overlaps'.

Outlining

To outline the designs, use a black fibre-tip pen. These come in a variety of widths and are available from stationers and art shops. As a general guide, choose a fine tip for small designs and a thicker tip for larger ones, although the choice will depend upon the effect you require: if only a small space is required for filling in with colour, outlining a small design with a thick tip would be an appropriate choice. Fibre-tip pens are also useful for filling in backgrounds and to produce various effects such as stoning and graining (see page 180).

BASIC PLOTTING TECHNIQUES

Curves and lines

All knotwork can be broken down into a series of curves and lines which make up the two basic units of all patterns plotted using this technique – hearts and loops. The curves are based on parts of a circle (i.e. quarter, half, three-quarter or full) and may be drawn either outside or inside the grid squares. Straight lines are drawn at angles of 45°, 90° or 180° to the vertical. (See Figs 2.2–2.4.)

FIG 2.2 Curves outside a square.

FIG 2.3 Curves inside a square.

FIG 2.4 Lines at 45°, 90° and 180° to the vertical.

Plotting the design

While there are various ways of plotting the curves to produce different effects, a general process can be applied to the plotting of all knotwork patterns. Following just the first two steps listed will produce the basic line work, and following all six will give a knotwork design of ribbons.

1 Plot all the curves.
2 Add the straight lines.
3 Apply ribbonwork by chosen
   method.
4 Identify crossing points for
   interweaving.
5 Ink in outlines.
6 Erase construction lines.

FIG 2.5 The two lines cross.

Draw the basic construction curves and
lines on graph paper. This drawing will
show the crossing points and also the
smallest space in the design, so the interweaving and appropriate width for the
ribbon can be determined. Once this has
been done, the lines can be converted to
ribbonwork.

FIG 2.6 The broken line indicates
that the vertical line passes underneath
the horizontal line.

Figure 2.30 shows four individual ribbons of equal width, which interweave.
The maximum thickness of these ribbons is determined by the size of the
centre square (the smallest space): half
the width of each ribbon = half the
width of the centre square.

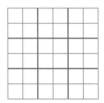

FIG 2.7 Four crossing lines.

Interweaving

Interweaving occurs when two lines
cross each other: one must pass over or
under the other. This is represented in
knotwork by breaking the line which
passes underneath. (See Figs 2.5 and
2.6.) Adding lines to the design increases the interweaving (see Figs 2.7 and
2.8), and when each line is joined
to another, a continuous line is produced (see Fig 2.9). There is no rule for

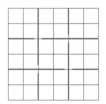

FIG 2.8 Broken lines indicate
which lines pass underneath.

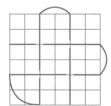

FIG 2.9 The four independent lines are
joined to form a continuous motif.

commencing the interweaving – the first line may be taken over or under as you choose. However, it is essential that once begun, the line is woven alternately over and under throughout the design. Never be tempted to move to another part of the design once you have begun as there is a real danger that the interweaving will be a disaster! In complicated designs, it is often easier to commence in the middle where the straight lines cross each other.

All lines must travel straight forward at each crossing point: they do not curve or alter their direction.

Ribbonwork

Ribbons are bands of a consistent width. In all ribbonwork, the complete width of each ribbon must be shown, so where two or more ribbons pass through a space, their combined width must not be greater than the width of that space. For this reason, the width of the ribbons is determined by the smallest available space in the design. (See Plotting the Design on page 9; see also Figs 2.27–2.30.)

There are two methods for creating ribbons – both start with the basic line work drawing.

METHOD 1

The first method is to draw lines on either side of the original lines, parallel

to the originals and equidistant from them. In simple patterns the crossing points can be easily identified (see Figs 2.10 and 2.11) and the ribbon can then be inked in following them. After inking the construction lines can be erased (see Figs 2.12 and 2.13).

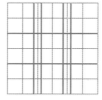

FIG 2.10 Lines are drawn either side of the original vertical lines, parallel to them.

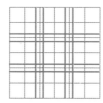

FIG 2.11 Parallel lines are drawn either side of the horizontal lines. Where these cross the vertical lines, interweaving will take place.

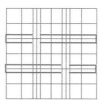

FIG 2.12 The horizontal ribbons are inked in following the interweaving shown in Fig 2.8.

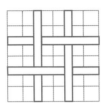

FIG **2.13** With the vertical lines inked in the ribbonwork is complete.

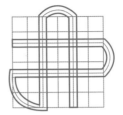

FIG **2.14** Converting Fig 2.9 to ribbonwork following Method 1.

METHOD 2

In more complex designs, the additional construction lines and points of intersection can be very confusing and difficult to follow. The second method for plotting ribbonwork helps to alleviate this by removing the lines at the crossing points. Rather than drawing in the new lines along the entire length of the original lines, lines on the inner side are drawn only up to the point where they meet the other new construction lines, as shown in Fig 2.15 (bordering the inside shapes), and a continuous line is drawn around the outer sides (bordering the edge). It is often simpler to complete the bordering in two or more stages, for example, bordering the lower edge before starting on the upper edge of the design. As with Method 1, all the new lines must be parallel to and equidistant from the original lines.

Figure 2.14 shows all the additional lines drawn in following Method 1, and Figs 2.15–2.18 show the plotting of ribbonwork following Method 2. Where

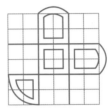

FIG **2.15** Filling in the inside shapes. The 'border' around each inside shape is half the width of the final ribbon.

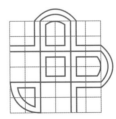

FIG **2.16** Bordering the upper edge. Again, the outside border is half the width of the final ribbon.

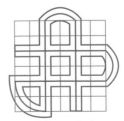

FIG **2.17** Bordering the lower edge.

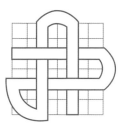

FIG 2.18 The completed
ribbonwork motif.

the construction of ribbonwork is shown in this book, it is done following Method 2. The bordering of inside shapes and outer edges is not shown for each design for reasons of space, but the process is the same in each case and can be applied to any design.

Double ribbons

Two ribbons drawn together, each finished in a different colour, create an interesting effect. As the interweaving for double ribbons is quite complicated, initial attempts at double ribbons should be worked on large squares.

Plotting is the same as for single ribbons (plotting the line drawing and bordering the inside shapes and edges), but what would be half a ribbon for single ribbons is treated as a whole ribbon for double ribbon work, and this affects the crossing points.

The interweaving of the first ribbon must be the opposite of that of the second, i.e. at a point where the first ribbon crosses over, the second ribbon must pass under and vice versa. Because the additional ribbon makes the interweaving more complicated, it is helpful to add guidelines to your pencil drawing to indicate where each ribbon will pass under at a crossing point. Complete the guidelines for one whole ribbon, passing

Plot and ink in the outline, then border the inside shapes and edges

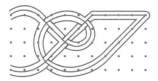

Add guidelines to indicate where the first ribbon passes under

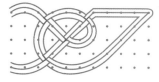

Add guidelines to indicate where the second ribbon passes under

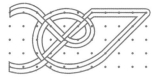

Ink in the first and then the second ribbon

Colour each ribbon

FIG 2.19 Plotting a double ribbon.

alternately over and under, before starting to mark the second. Remember that whatever pattern you have chosen for the first ribbon, the pattern for the second will be the opposite.

With the interweaving indicated, ink in first one ribbon, and then the other. (See Fig 2.19.)

Split ribbon technique

By extending one or more branches from the main ribbon, the artist can weave these strands independently, before joining them to the main branch again, as shown in Figs 2.20 and 2.21. This allows addi-

tional and more complicated interlacing. The technique is also very effective in creating corner motifs, as it enables the interlacing to be contained within a border frame of a suitable shape. (See Chapter 13, Corner Motifs.)

FIG 2.22 An example of a split ribbon motif.

Plotting the motif

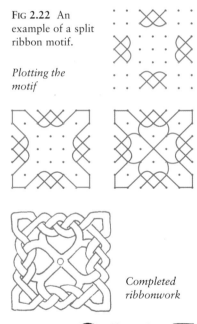

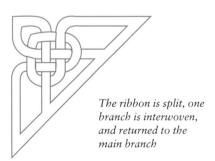

The ribbon is split, one branch is interwoven, and returned to the main branch

FIG 2.20 Splitting the ribbon allows additional interweaving.

Completed ribbonwork

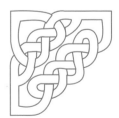

Two branches are extended from the main branch, interwoven, and rejoined in the main branch

FIG 2.21 Border frames can be created with the split ribbon technique.

The motif repeated and coloured

Mitred corners

Lengths of knotwork borders and panels can be joined at a mitred corner to form a frame (see Fig 2.23). A useful method of working out a mitred corner is as follows:

1 Draw the knot to be tested, in pencil, on graph paper.

2 On a piece of scrap graph paper draw the same knot, in ink, and cut it out. Do not leave any border around the knotwork lines.

3 Place the cut-out knot at 90° to the pencilled knot. This will show clearly the number of ends that are to be joined.

4 Try various ways of joining these ends by moving the cut-out knot nearer to, and further away from, the pencilled knot. (See Fig 2.24.)

FIG 2.23 A complete frame, with mitred corners.

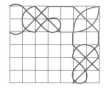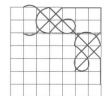

FIG 2.24 Examples of joining panels to form a mitred corner.

General plotting tips

1 Use large squares until you are comfortable with interweaving, and for complex designs use 1cm squares to clarify the crossing points.

2 Avoid square and pointed corners in ribbonwork unless they are required to create an effect. Although the initial design is plotted using sharp corners, they should be rounded before inking in the design. (See Figs 2.25 and 2.26.)

3 In patterns where a sharp corner is part of the design, round off the inside border to create a softer effect.

4 In ribbonwork, the width of the ribbon is determined by the smallest space in the design. It is essential to keep the ribbon width as uniform as possible.

5 When dealing with tight spaces, do not attempt to draw all the lines within the space. Instead, place a dot in the centre of the space to act as a guide. (See Figs 2.27–2.30.)

6 Complex designs can be difficult to ink in once the ribbon has been sketched. In such cases it is helpful to make a simple line drawing in a larger scale before attempting the actual working, so that the crossing points can be easily identified.

7 When a design is required to fill a specific area, divide the space into squares and select a suitable knot from any section. For example, an area of 5.5 x 2.5cm will accommodate a design requiring 11 x 5 squares, using 5mm squares. Remember to measure slightly within the area available to accommodate the outside of the ribbon.

FIG 2.25 Rounding off the pointed
corners to give a softer effect.

FIG 2.26 The softening effect of rounded
corners shown in ribbonwork.

FIG 2.27 Mark the centre of
the square with a dot.

FIG 2.28 Add all the inside
ribbon edges.

FIG 2.29 Add all the outside
ribbon edges.

FIG 2.30 The completed ribbonwork
showing interweaving.

PART TWO

---◆---

The Designs

Hearts

Hearts are created by plotting curves and straight lines. They can be adapted and embellished by extending diagonal lines from their centre, extending the base and extending the top.

---◆---

Hearts can be plotted in one of four ways:

a   *b*   *c*   *d*

a

With the lower part of the heart
drawn as a semicircle

b

With the base of the heart forming
an angle of 90°

c

With a semicircular base, but plotted
diagonally (i.e. the midline of the heart runs
diagonally through the plotting square)

d

With a right-angled base,
plotted diagonally

Chapter 3

Small Hearts

All the designs in this section are constructed by plotting small hearts and extending diagonal lines from the centre of each heart to produce variations in design and interweaving.

1

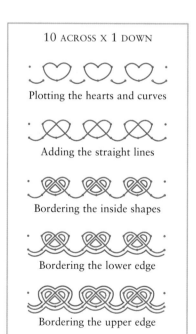

10 ACROSS X 1 DOWN

Plotting the hearts and curves

Adding the straight lines

Bordering the inside shapes

Bordering the lower edge

Bordering the upper edge

Hearts are plotted one square apart, and lines are extended from the centre of each to join the hearts into a knotted ribbon. Don't worry if your initial attempts produce a narrow ribbon – this is quite normal, and as your confidence increases, you will soon be able to regulate the width. It is sometimes an advantage to use narrow ribbons, especially at points where there is close interweaving.

2

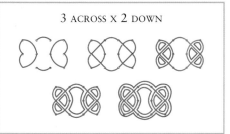

3 ACROSS X 2 DOWN

A small, decorative knot constructed by placing two hearts base to base.

3

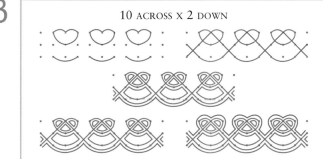

10 ACROSS X 2 DOWN

This design also plots hearts one square apart, however, the diagonals are extended over two squares, resulting in two interwoven ribbons. If the loose ends are then joined, the border is made continuous. (Design 13 is a variation of this border.)

4

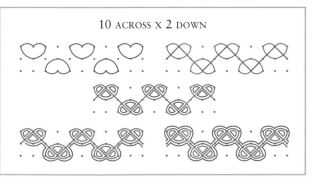

10 ACROSS X 2 DOWN

Although the hearts are plotted in a slightly different way from Design 3, the diagonals are treated in exactly the same way. This design, together with Design 6, has a double row of hearts in which the diagonals produce a variation of Design 1.

5

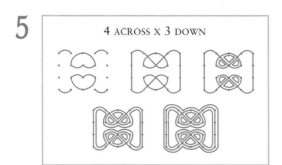

4 ACROSS X 3 DOWN

Placing the hearts facing towards each other produces longer side loops which can be slightly softened by twisting (as in Design 7).

6

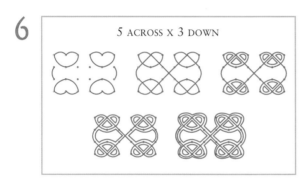

5 ACROSS X 3 DOWN

A pair of hearts plotted one square apart, base to base. The diagonals are joined across the centre and linked together at the sides into a continuous motif.

7

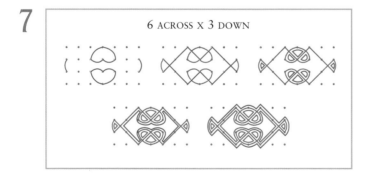

6 ACROSS X 3 DOWN

Two hearts plotted facing towards each other in the same way as Design 5, but decorated with twists in the side loops.

8

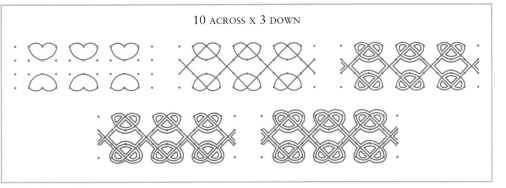

10 ACROSS X 3 DOWN

Hearts are placed base to base as for Design 6, but the diagonals are extended to produce a border design.

9

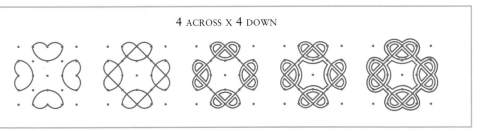

4 ACROSS X 4 DOWN

Hearts are plotted at 90° to each other which gives a design that will fill a square.

10

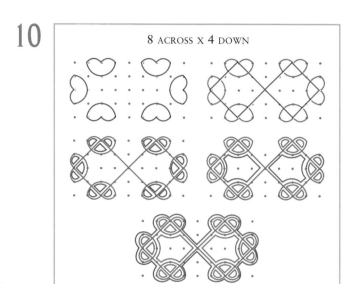

8 ACROSS X 4 DOWN

This variation of Design 9 extends parallel sides of the framework to produce a rectangular motif.

11

8 ACROSS X 4 DOWN

This motif can be adapted into a ribbon border by plotting several motifs and joining the side loops.

12

5 ACROSS X 5 DOWN

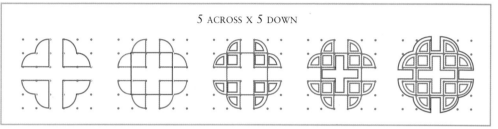

A variation of Design 9, with the hearts plotted diagonally, and their bases pointed.

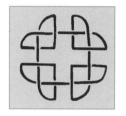 

13

14 ACROSS X 5 DOWN

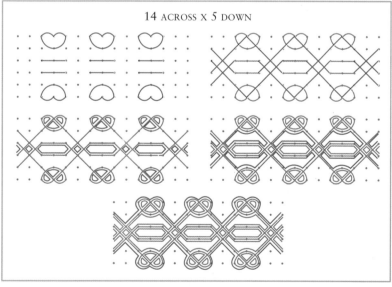

A variation of Design 3. Each row of hearts is plotted two squares apart, with a space of three squares between the rows. Diagonals are extended through three squares and interlaced.

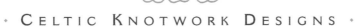
14

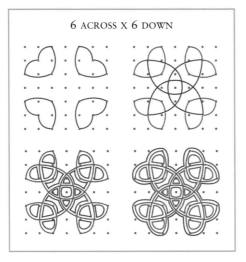

6 ACROSS X 6 DOWN

There is some tight knotting in the centre of both this design and Design 18. To avoid mistakes in the lacing, try using 1cm squares for your first attempt.

15

7 ACROSS X 6 DOWN

Two interwoven motifs, each one a variation of Design 2. The bases are plotted three squares apart and the diagonals extended over two squares.

16

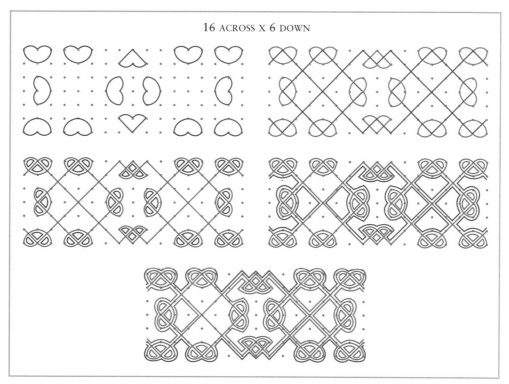

16 ACROSS X 6 DOWN

A variation of Design 9 in which the four heart motifs are plotted further apart. This allows the long diagonals, extending from the rows of inverted hearts, to be interwoven.

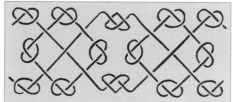

17

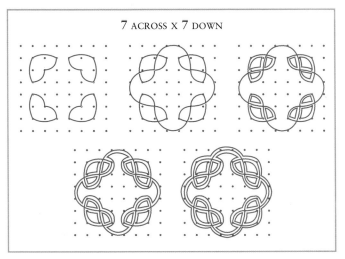

7 ACROSS X 7 DOWN

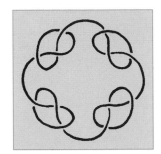

The hearts are plotted diagonally, facing inwards, to produce a circular design, as has also been done in Design 19. Once the framework has been sketched in, the angles are rounded off to soften the effect.

18

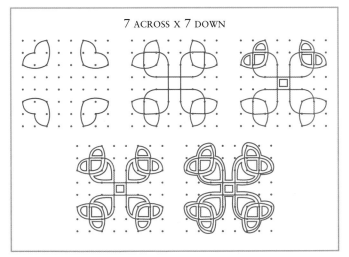

7 ACROSS X 7 DOWN

Another design in which there is a tightly woven centre. Use 1cm paper to try this design and make sure that there is sufficient room left in the centre for adding the ribbon.

19

25 ACROSS X 7 DOWN

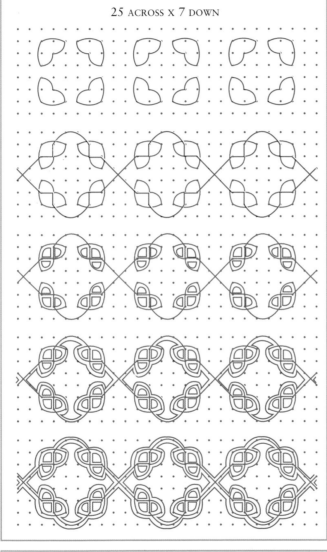

Design 17 is developed into a border by extending the sides. Join the ends together for a continuous border.

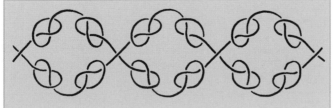

20

8 ACROSS X 8 DOWN

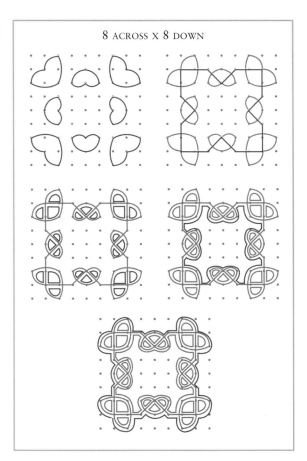

Hearts are plotted at 45° and 90° to the vertical to give a continuous motif.

21

10 ACROSS X 8 DOWN

A variation of Design 15 with the pairs of hearts plotted further apart.

22

10 ACROSS X 8 DOWN

This panel can be adapted into a deep border by plotting several panels and joining them together using the side loops.

A fine example of the ancient Derbyshire custom of decorating wells with pictures made
from flowers and leaves.

Chapter 4

Large Hearts

Compare these designs to those in Chapter 3. They have been drawn using the same size square, but the interweaving is much tighter. For this reason, I recommend using a larger square for the initial test piece so that the crossing points and interweaving can be seen more clearly. The base of the small heart is deeper to allow more interweaving in the centre. It is plotted in one of three styles: a deep curve, a shallow curve, or pointed.

23

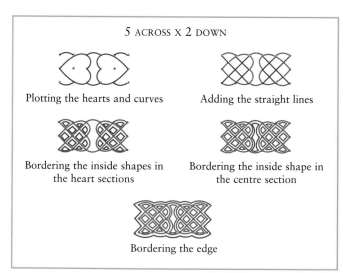

5 ACROSS X 2 DOWN

Plotting the hearts and curves

Adding the straight lines

Bordering the inside shapes in the heart sections

Bordering the inside shape in the centre section

Bordering the edge

The small motif is a continuous line.

24

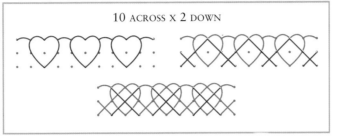

10 ACROSS X 2 DOWN

In this border, three ribbons of hearts are interwoven.

25

18 ACROSS X 2 DOWN

Pairs of hearts are interwoven with two ribbons to form a border design.

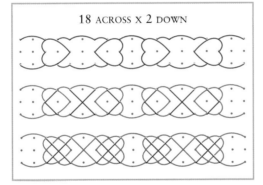

26

6 ACROSS X 3 DOWN

The four diagonals in the centre of the heart are extended over three squares and joined together in pairs. The two additional top diagonals are curved around the large heart and joined together at the base. This motif is continuous.

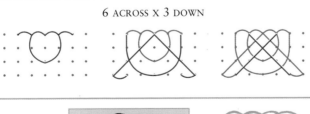

27

14 ACROSS X 3 DOWN

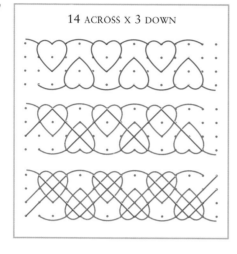

A border of interwoven lines of hearts.

28

5 ACROSS X 4 DOWN

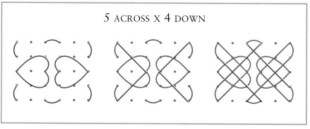

In this variation of Design 26, the hearts are plotted facing inwards. The additional diagonals at the top are extended over one square and joined with a twist.

29

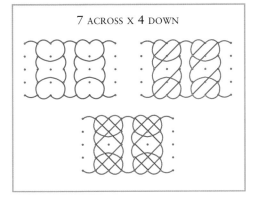

7 ACROSS X 4 DOWN

Two interwoven heart ribbons.
Join the ends for a continuous line.

30

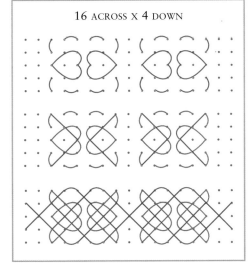

16 ACROSS X 4 DOWN

An extension of Design 28 in which
individual motifs are interwoven into
a border design.

31

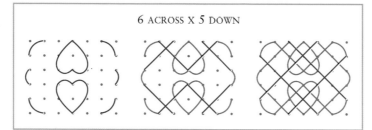

6 ACROSS X 5 DOWN

A closely interwoven, continuous ribbon.

32

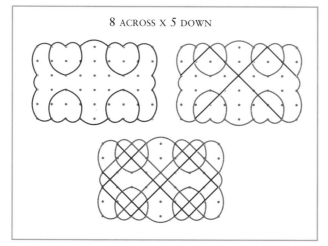

8 ACROSS X 5 DOWN

Plotting the hearts further apart leaves more space across the centre for interweaving.

33

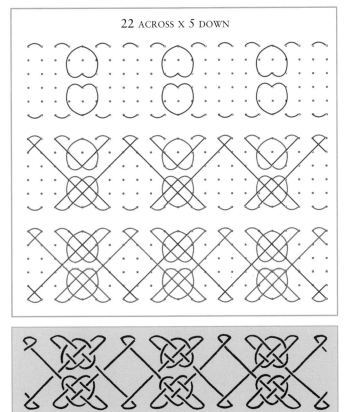

22 ACROSS X 5 DOWN

Two interlaced ribbons. Join the ends for a continuous line.

34

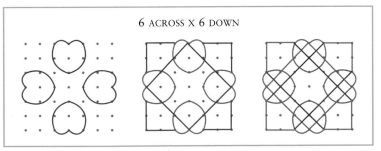

6 ACROSS X 6 DOWN

A variation of Design 9 (see Small Hearts, page 25), in which the hearts are interwoven with two links.

35

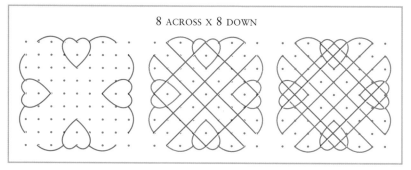

8 ACROSS X 8 DOWN

An extension of Design 34
in which the hearts are
interwoven with four links.

36

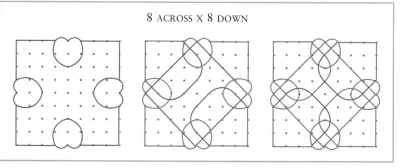

8 ACROSS X 8 DOWN

Although this design appears
to be continuous, it is a
combination of four separate
links interwoven with the
diagonals of four hearts.

37

9 ACROSS X 9 DOWN

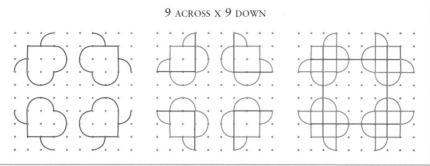

Hearts plotted
diagonally and laced
into a continuous motif.

38

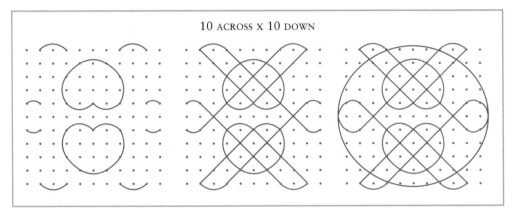

10 ACROSS X 10 DOWN

A variation of Design 28. As an alternative to twisting
the diagonals together, they are interlaced and taken
round the base of each heart, in a semicircle.

A classic knot design adapted to suit the craft of quilling.

Chapter 5

EXTENDING THE BASE

---◆---

In this section, the heart is plotted with a pointed base which is then extended to provide two extra diagonals. Connecting the bases of hearts reduces the length of the diagonals and side loops. Interweaving becomes tighter and although the squares are the same size as in previous sections, the designs appear smaller.

39

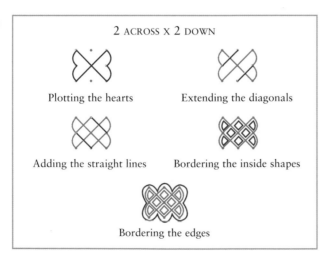

2 ACROSS X 2 DOWN

Plotting the hearts

Extending the diagonals

Adding the straight lines

Bordering the inside shapes

Bordering the edges

In this design, two hearts are joined at the base, and the diagonal lines taken from the centre of each heart are joined to make a continuous motif.

40

5 ACROSS X 2 DOWN

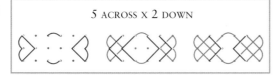

Here the hearts are plotted further apart and the base extensions from each are used to join the hearts together. Diagonals are extended from the centre of each heart in the usual way and then brought back diagonally to meet at the base. The motif is continuous.

41

4 ACROSS X 4 DOWN

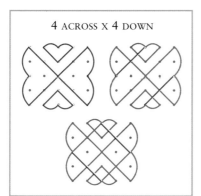

A variation of Design 39 in which the bases of two hearts are joined and the diagonals from the centre of each are combined with a small heart for additional decoration. The motif is continuous.

42

8 ACROSS X 4 DOWN

This continuous motif appears to be more complex, but it is plotted from two large hearts which are joined together at the base. Where the diagonals from the centre of the hearts meet, the ribbons are decorated with a small heart, and the same treatment is given to the additional diagonals which are extended above the large hearts and meet together in a further small heart.

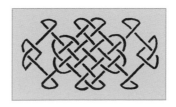

43

14 ACROSS X 4 DOWN

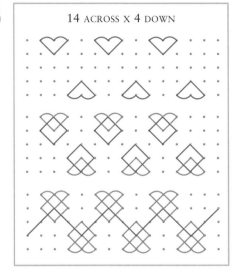

A variation of Design 40 to produce a continuous border.

44

19 ACROSS X 4 DOWN

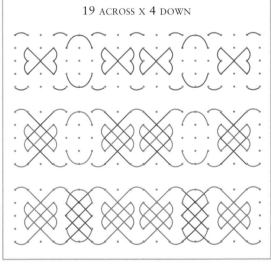

Although this design appears to be continuous, it is a series of individual motifs which are interlaced with a figure of 8 to form a border.

45

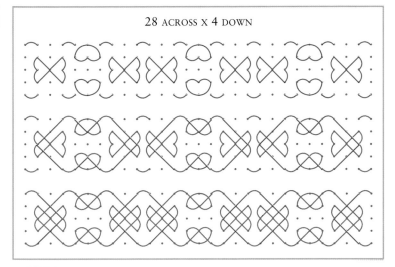

28 ACROSS X 4 DOWN

A border of two interwoven motifs, the ends of which may be joined together to make a continuous ribbon.

46

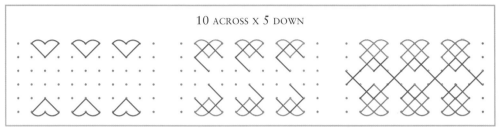

10 ACROSS X 5 DOWN

A variation of Design 43. Join the ends
together for a continuous ribbon.

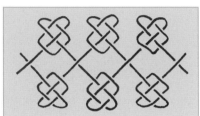

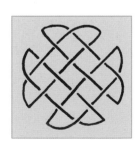

47

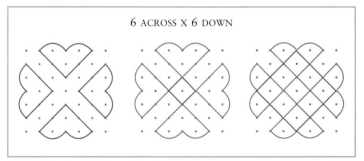

6 ACROSS X 6 DOWN

The extended bases of this design produce
four interwoven links.

48

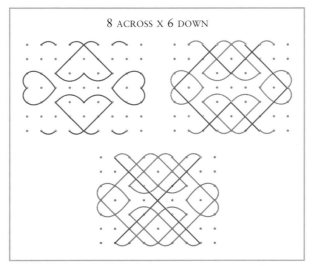

8 ACROSS X 6 DOWN

A continuous ribbon in which the large hearts are plotted facing each other and the extended bases meet in a small heart for additional decoration.

49

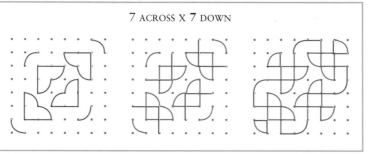

7 ACROSS X 7 DOWN

A very simple design which is plotted diagonally. The extended bases are looped to give a picot effect to the continuous motif. If the grid is plotted diagonally, the motif will appear rectangular on the page.

50

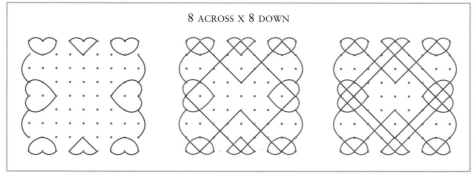

8 ACROSS X 8 DOWN

Both small and large hearts are combined here to produce a continuous motif.

51

8 ACROSS X 8 DOWN

A variation of Design 45 in which individual motifs are laced together to form a border design.

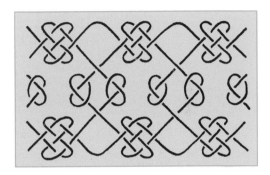

Chapter 6

Extending the Top

Many of the designs produced by extending the top of the heart are individual woven links. The squares remain the same size, but the additional interweaving around the outside of the designs makes them appear larger.

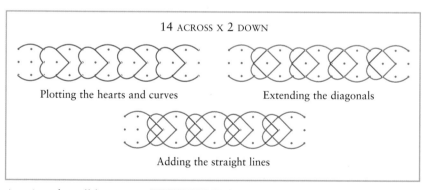

14 ACROSS X 2 DOWN

Plotting the hearts and curves

Extending the diagonals

Adding the straight lines

A series of small heart motifs are linked into a border design.

53

4 ACROSS X 3 DOWN

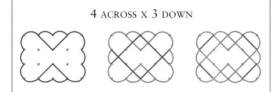

A continuous motif using two small hearts as the foundation.

54

6 ACROSS X 3 DOWN

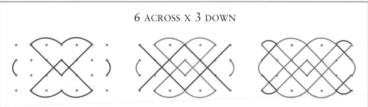

Two hearts are plotted with their bases overlapping. The top of each heart is extended and interwoven with the diagonals extended from the other. The motif is continuous.

55

6 ACROSS X 4 DOWN

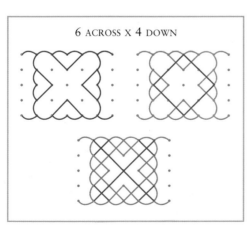

Three interwoven links are laced with two ribbons to create a border design. The ends of the ribbons can be joined together at the beginning and end of the border.

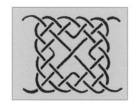

56

6 ACROSS X 4 DOWN

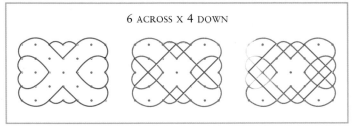

Four hearts, two large and two small, form
the basis of this continuous ribbon.

57

14 ACROSS X 4 DOWN

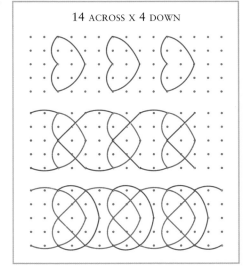

A border which is composed of individual
heart motifs in which the top extensions are
joined together under the base of the heart.

58

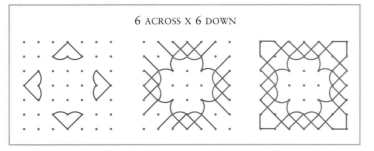

6 ACROSS X 6 DOWN

The central motif has four branches which are interwoven with two links.

59

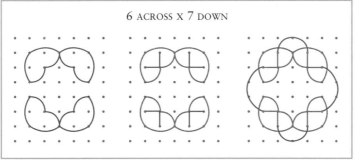

6 ACROSS X 7 DOWN

A variation of Design 17 (see Small Hearts, page 30). The motif is continuous.

60

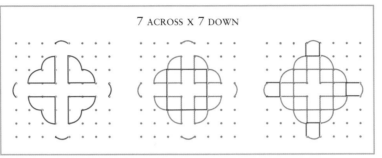

7 ACROSS X 7 DOWN

A variation of Design 12 (see Small Hearts, page 27) in which the hearts, plotted in a square formation, have the tops extended into a design of three interwoven links.

61

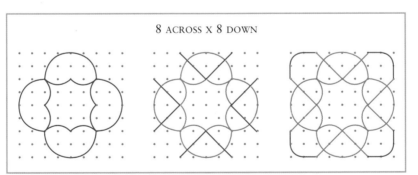

8 ACROSS X 8 DOWN

The tops of the hearts are interwoven in this motif. The ribbonwork for this design shows the corners 'squared off'.

62

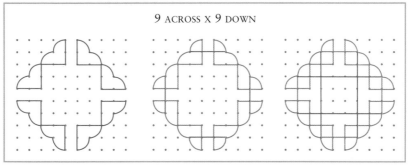

9 ACROSS X 9 DOWN

A variation of Design 60 in which there are two hearts on each side of the square. Interweaving takes place in the centre of the design and the motif is made up of four interwoven links.

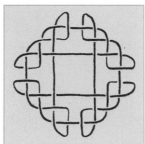

63

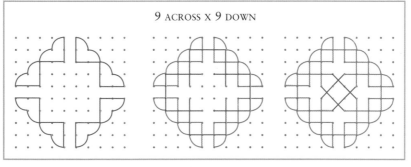

9 ACROSS X 9 DOWN

In this variation of Design 62, the diagonals interweave across the centre to produce a continuous motif.

Chapter 7

EXTENDING THE BASE & TOP

◆

This is the final section developed from the heart. Lines are extended from the centre, top and base to provide more ribbons for interlacing. As there are so many crossing points in the ribbons, ensure that the test piece is plotted on large squares so that these points are clear and the design can be followed through correctly.

64

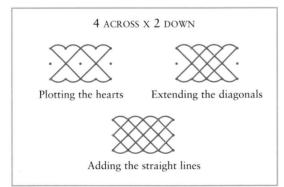

4 ACROSS X 2 DOWN

Plotting the hearts   Extending the diagonals

Adding the straight lines

This is an example of plaitwork in which both the top and base of the heart are extended and the only curved areas are around the edge of the design, with regular interweaving across the centre.

65

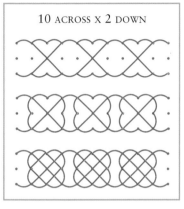

Motifs of two small, interwoven links laced together with two ribbons into a border design.

66

10 ACROSS X 3 DOWN

The extension of both the top and base of the heart in this design forms two interwoven links through which further ribbons pass. The ends of the ribbons can be joined together.

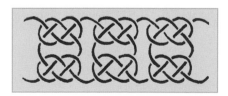

67

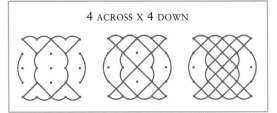

4 ACROSS X 4 DOWN

A continuous ribbon which can easily be converted into a border by extending the side loops outwards diagonally, allowing them to cross over each other instead of joining them together.

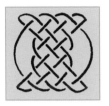

68

5 ACROSS X 4 DOWN

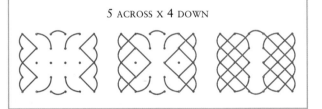

This continuous motif can be converted to a border by rotating it 90° and extending the ribbons diagonally, allowing them to cross as for Design 67.

69

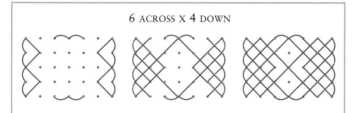

6 ACROSS X 4 DOWN

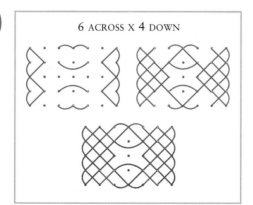

A continuous motif in which adjacent hearts are plotted and their bases extended into a point to resemble a large heart with four upper curves. There is close weaving within each large heart and only one pair of diagonals across the centre.

70

6 ACROSS X 4 DOWN

A variation of Design 69 in which hearts are plotted in the same way, but the diagonals do not cross in the centre. The motif is continuous.

71

6 ACROSS X 4 DOWN

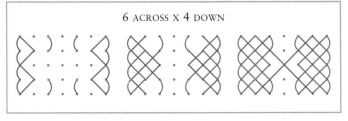

The hearts are plotted as for Designs 69 and 70, but the two motifs are joined only across the centre of the design, the diagonals being looped back across the centre.

72

7 ACROSS X 4 DOWN

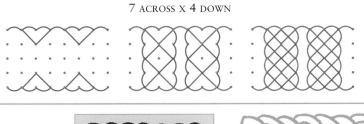

A deep border design of two interwoven ribbons plotted from small hearts, the bases of which are two squares apart.

73

10 ACROSS X 4 DOWN

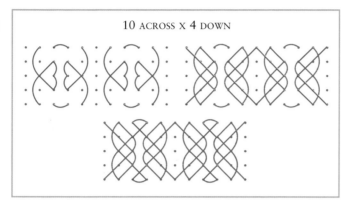

Small hearts plotted one square apart with the tops facing inwards are developed into a border design of two ribbons. A twist has been added at the top and bottom between each pair of hearts.

74

6 ACROSS X 4 DOWN

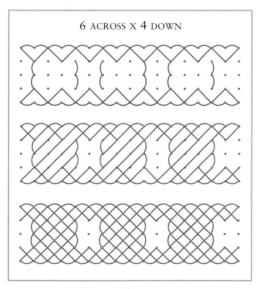

In this motif the diagonals are curved back towards the design instead of being joined straight across the centre.

75

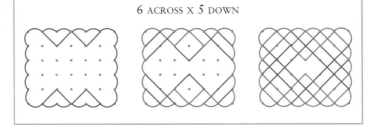

6 ACROSS X 5 DOWN

The bases of two hearts are extended into a large heart with four top curves. The motif is continuous.

76

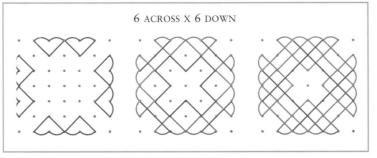

6 ACROSS X 6 DOWN

A heart motif interwoven with two links.

 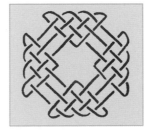 

77

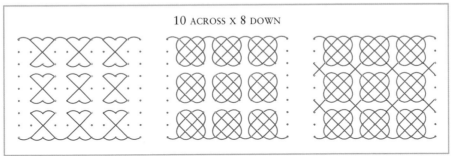

10 ACROSS X 8 DOWN

An extension of Design 65 in which the small motifs are linked into a larger panel.

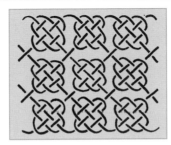

78

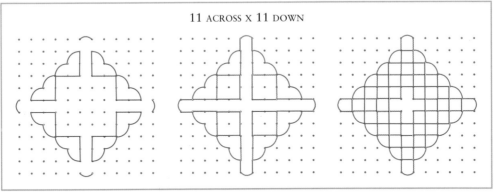

11 ACROSS X 11 DOWN

Four pairs of hearts developed into a group of four interwoven links by extending the diagonals and tops.

Loops

The loop is a variation of a heart – half the top remains, but the other half is free to travel in any direction, opening up greater possibilities for designs, particularly with borders.

◆

There are four ways of plotting loops:

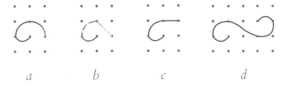

a   *b*   *c*   *d*

a
Attaching the loop to a half circle

b
Attaching one end of the loop to a quarter circle and
the other to a straight line plotted at 45° to the vertical

c
Attaching one end of the loop to a quarter circle and
the other to a straight line plotted at 90° to the vertical

d
Attaching a loop each to two quarter circles and
joining the two with a straight line

Chapter 8

Small Loops

---◆---

The small loop is extremely versatile: many of the designs can be combined and loose ends can be joined together in pairs. Although Design 104 is mainly straight lines, it has been included in this section as the basic plotting is worked from a small loop.

79

8 ACROSS X 2 DOWN

Plotting the loops   Adding diagonals   Adding straight lines

The small loops are plotted with the centres joined and the lower part of the loop extended over four squares. There are two ribbons in the design which may be joined at the ends to complete the border.

80

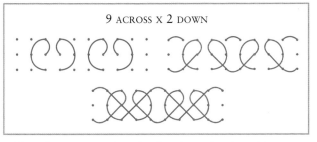

9 ACROSS X 2 DOWN

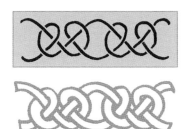

Although it appears that this border is developed from pairs of hearts plotted facing towards each other it is, in fact, two interwoven ribbons.

81

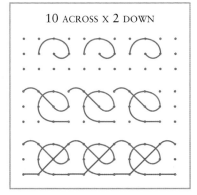

10 ACROSS X 2 DOWN

A simple border design of two interwoven ribbons, with the small loops plotted one square apart.

82

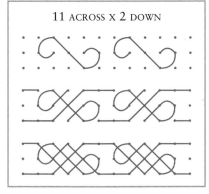

11 ACROSS X 2 DOWN

Two interwoven ribbons in which the diagonals of the loops form the centre diagonals of the completed ribbons.

83

15 ACROSS X 2 DOWN

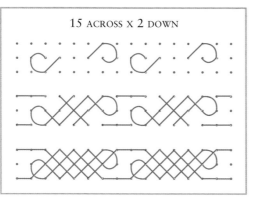

A variation of Design 82 in which the small loops are plotted further apart to allow more interweaving between the diagonals of each knot.

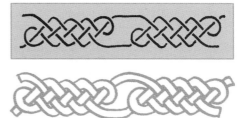

84

17 ACROSS X 2 DOWN

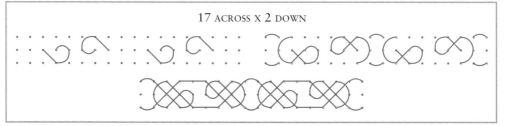

A border design of two interwoven ribbons in which a half circle is used to turn the diagonal back and through the small loop.

85

7 ACROSS X 3 DOWN

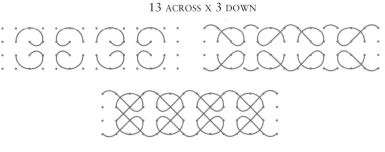

The free ends of each pair of loops are joined and the diagonals extended in this small, continuous motif.

86

13 ACROSS X 3 DOWN

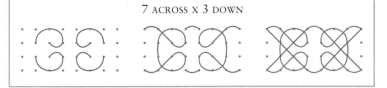

The plotting of this border is the same as for Design 85, but the free end here is extended and used to join the motif into a border of two interwoven ribbons.

87

13 ACROSS X 3 DOWN

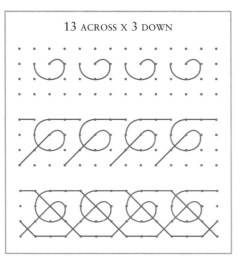

A variation of Design 81 in which the diagonals are extended to allow more inter-weaving between the motifs. There is a repeat of three interwoven ribbons in this design.

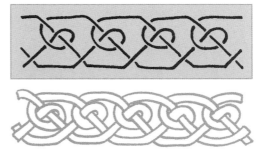

88

16 ACROSS X 3 DOWN

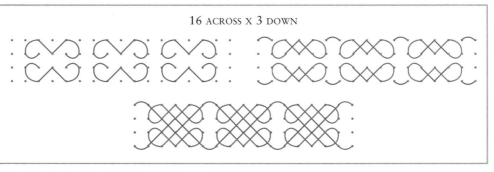

A further design in which it would appear that the border is a repeat of individual interwoven motifs. It is, in fact, two ribbons which interweave in the centre of each motif.

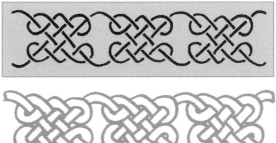

89

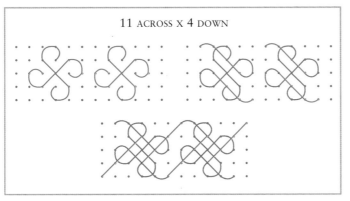

11 ACROSS X 4 DOWN

There are two interwoven ribbons in this design which are connected by drawing the free end of one pair of small loops through the loops of the other pair.

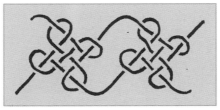 

90

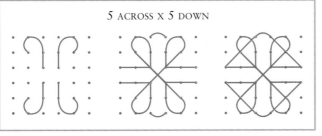 

5 ACROSS X 5 DOWN

A small, continuous motif which can be developed into a border design (see Design 96).

91

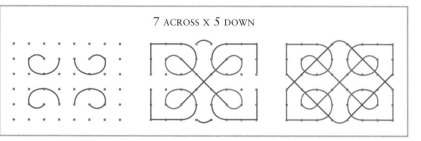

7 ACROSS X 5 DOWN

A simple, continuous motif developed from four small loops. This design could be developed into a border by extending the lines at the top and bottom as an alternative to joining them, as shown here.

92

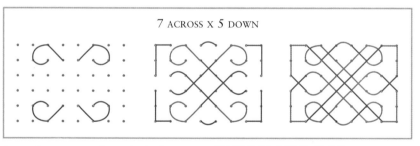

7 ACROSS X 5 DOWN

A continuous motif in which there is a small amount of interweaving in the centre.

93

9 ACROSS X 5 DOWN

A deeper border design which is a variation of Design 80. Two rows of small loops are plotted and connected by the free end of each loop. There are four ribbons in this design, the ends of which can be joined in pairs to complete the border.

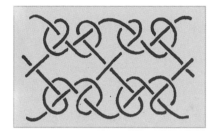

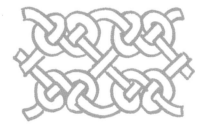

94

12 ACROSS X 5 DOWN

Four ribbons interweave in this design, each one having a pattern of two small loops and a long ribbon which passes through the loop and diagonal of another.

95

13 ACROSS X 5 DOWN

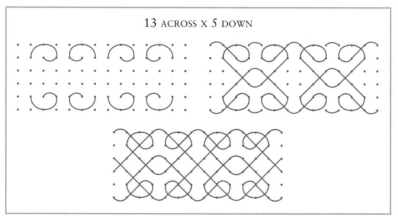

Small loops are plotted in pairs, one row at the top of the design and one row at the bottom. The two rows are interwoven into a knotwork border by using two further ribbons which travel through the loops, crossing between each motif.

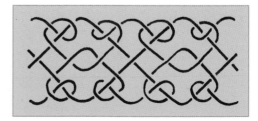

96

13 ACROSS X 5 DOWN

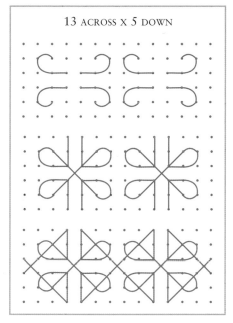

Design 90 developed into a border design. Although there are two interwoven ribbons, the ends may be joined together to make the design continuous.

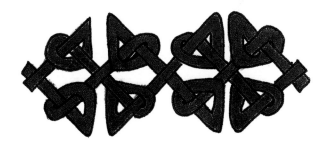

97

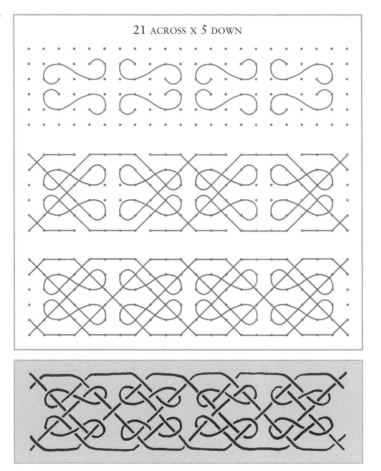

21 ACROSS X 5 DOWN

There are four ribbons in this border which is developed from pairs of small loops connected by interwoven ribbons.

98

6 ACROSS X 6 DOWN

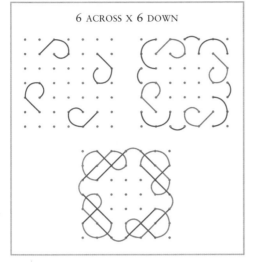

A variation of Design 84 to form a continuous motif which can be used as a frame.

99

15 ACROSS X 6 DOWN

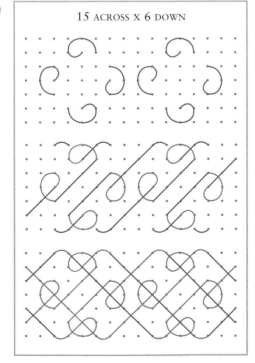

A border design of four interwoven ribbons in which the free ends of the loops of each are joined together on the diagonal before interweaving with another ribbon.

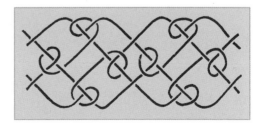

100

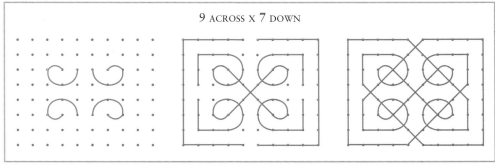

9 ACROSS X 7 DOWN

Plotted as for Design 91, the free end of each loop is further extended to form a double border.

101

8 ACROSS X 8 DOWN

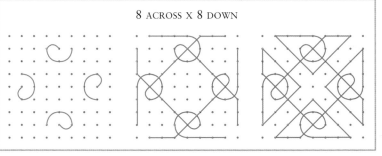

This design is an example of filling in the corner spaces by using long points.

102

9 ACROSS X 9 DOWN

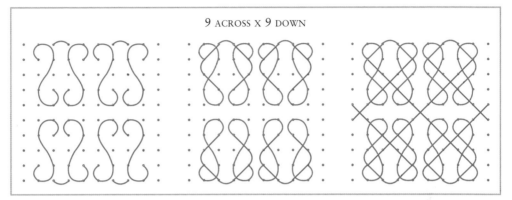

A deep border of two interwoven ribbons, each one developed from pairs of connected loops repeating alternately at the top and bottom of the design.

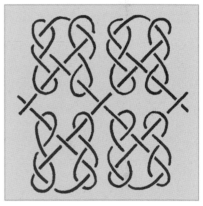

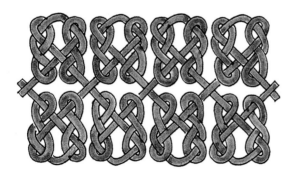

103

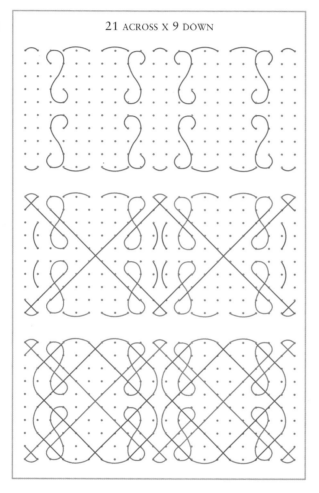

21 ACROSS X 9 DOWN

A series of small, connected loops with a twist between each pair. The long diagonals of each pair interweave with each other and between the two links which envelop the looped ribbons.

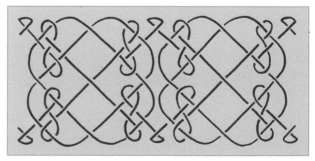

104

13 ACROSS X 13 DOWN

Small loops, plotted in pairs on each side of a square, interweave with curved and straight lines to form a continuous motif.

85

Chapter 9

LARGE LOOPS

---◆---

A large loop is an extension of a small loop. This produces longer ribbons between the outer interweavings. Most large loop borders can be developed from small loops by plotting them three squares apart to allow for the extra length of ribbon. In many large loop designs a point can be introduced to add interest.

105

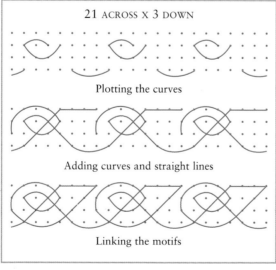

21 ACROSS X 3 DOWN

Plotting the curves

Adding curves and straight lines

Linking the motifs

A continuous border of large loops, the initial plotting taken over three squares to give a spherical shape.

106

25 ACROSS X 3 DOWN

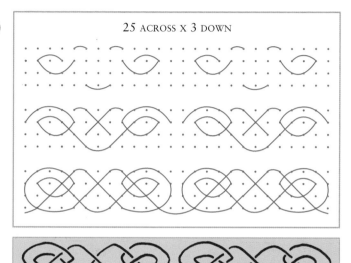

A variation of Design 105 in which the large loops are plotted in pairs, with additional interweaving between each pair.

107

28 ACROSS X 3 DOWN

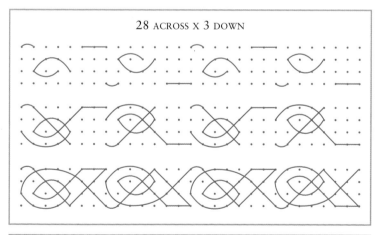

A further variation of Design 105 in which the large loops are plotted alternately down and up. The points at the outer edge turn back to interweave through the loop. The ribbon is continuous.

108

11 ACROSS X 4 DOWN

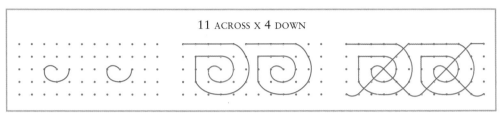

A border of two interwoven ribbons showing one
motif with a point and one with the normal curve.

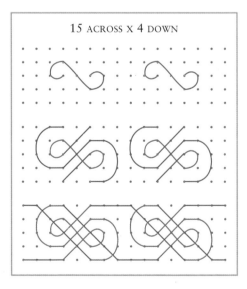

109

15 ACROSS X 4 DOWN

This pattern is constructed using a base of
small loops, increasing the spacing from one
square to three.

110

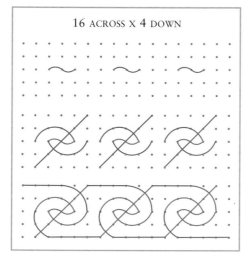

16 ACROSS X 4 DOWN

A further example of using a small loop to plot large loops. Here the small loop ribbon is interwoven with a second ribbon which gives the impression of a large loop design.

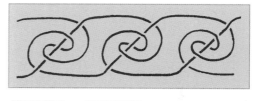

111

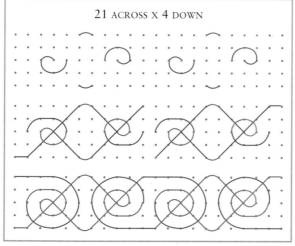

21 ACROSS X 4 DOWN

These two interwoven ribbons show an alternative plotting of the small loop which is then extended into a large loop.

112

16 ACROSS X 5 DOWN

The loop is turned three times before changing direction in a sharp point and travelling back down through the loop.

113

9 ACROSS X 7 DOWN

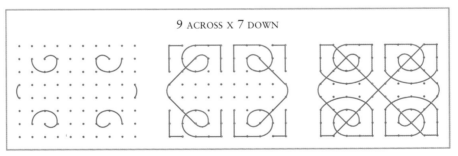

Small loops are plotted base to base in a square formation, with two squares between each. Ribbons are taken in the normal way from the centre of the remaining 'heart' and the free end is taken round into a point before circling back under the original loops. This continuous motif can be developed into a border by extending the side lines rather than joining them into a small curve.

114

13 ACROSS X 9 DOWN

Plotting the initial part of the loop over three squares allows a spherical shape. In this continuous motif the centre of each loop is taken diagonally across the centre to join the loops together in pairs.

115

17 ACROSS X 9 DOWN

A variation of Design 113 in which the motifs are rotated at 45° to the vertical. The four ribbons can be joined into pairs.

116

14 ACROSS X 10 DOWN

A variation of Design 114. The motif is continuous, and the sides of the design are decorated with twists.

Chapter 10

EXTENDED LOOPS

◆

Extended loops are hearts which do not meet in the centre. This creates an alternative method of joining heart designs as motifs and borders: the space can either be filled with an additional curve or used to extend lines through the top of the heart.

117

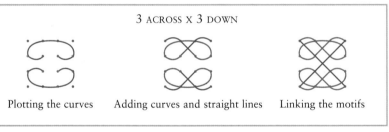

3 ACROSS X 3 DOWN

Plotting the curves Adding curves and straight lines Linking the motifs

In this continuous motif the centre square is used to allow two lines to cross between the top of the hearts.

118

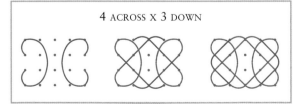

4 ACROSS X 3 DOWN

A simple motif of two hearts interlinked by extending lines through the top space.

119

5 ACROSS X 3 DOWN

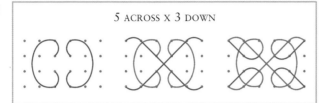

This continuous motif is an example of how a design can be achieved by an alternative method of plotting. In this section it is developed from two extended loops, but four small loops would have been equally satisfactory.

120

13 ACROSS X 3 DOWN

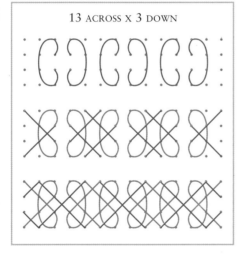

Individual heart motifs interlinked to form a border design.

121

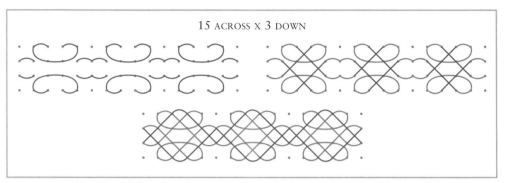

15 ACROSS X 3 DOWN

Two ribbons of continuous hearts interlink
in the centre of this border.

122

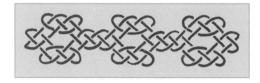

5 ACROSS X 4 DOWN

A variation of Design 121 to make a motif.
This motif includes a heart base extension.

123

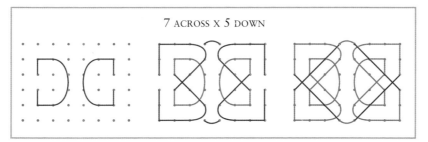

7 ACROSS X 5 DOWN

The outer edges of the heart motif
are pointed for a different effect.

124

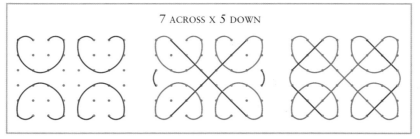

7 ACROSS X 5 DOWN

Compare this design with Design 6
(see Small Hearts, page 24).
The extended loop gives a larger,
bolder design.

125

13 ACROSS X 5 DOWN

Another variation of Design 121, this one linking individual motifs to produce a border design.

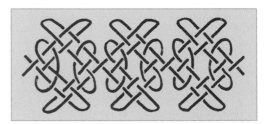

126

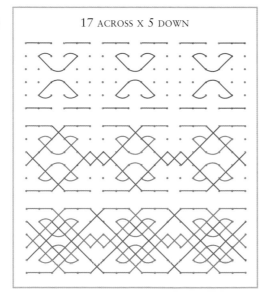

17 ACROSS X 5 DOWN

A more complex border in which six heart ribbons are interlinked.

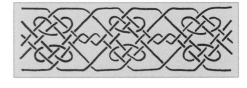

127

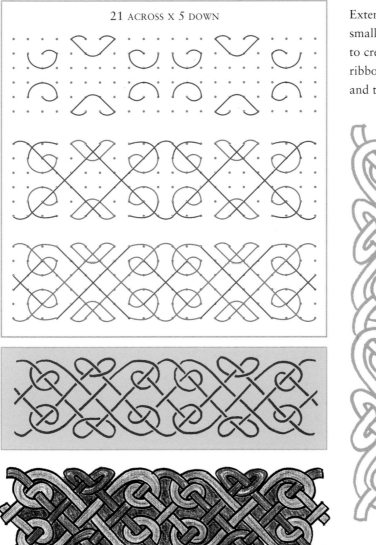

21 ACROSS X 5 DOWN

Extended hearts and small loops interweave to create a border of four ribbons, i.e. two hearts and two small loops.

128

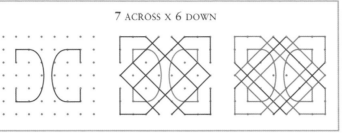

7 ACROSS X 6 DOWN

A further motif with angled corners in which two ribbons interweave.

129

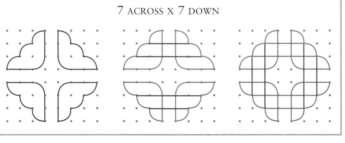

7 ACROSS X 7 DOWN

A large heart motif interwoven with a square link.

130

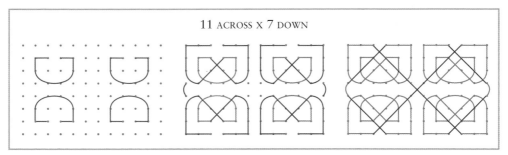

11 ACROSS X 7 DOWN

A variation of Design 123 in which the motifs are plotted one square apart and interwoven with the diagonals from the outer edge of each.

131

15 ACROSS X 7 DOWN

A large border design in which six individual heart ribbons interweave.

132

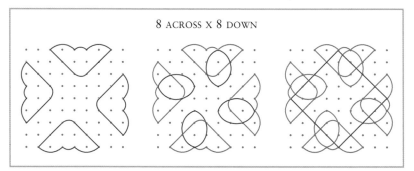

8 ACROSS X 8 DOWN

Continuous motif in which the additional space is used to create an extra loop at the base of the heart.

133

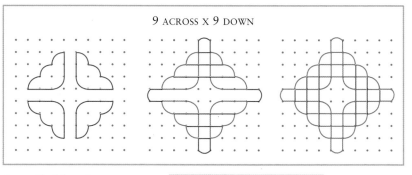

9 ACROSS X 9 DOWN

A motif of four interwoven links which is plotted by extending the top of the loops in the same way that the top of the small heart was extended.

134

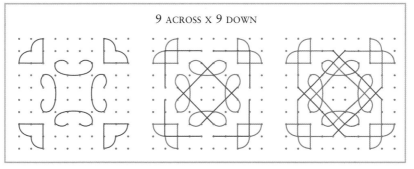

9 ACROSS X 9 DOWN

Four loops are plotted
backing each other in a
square formation. The
diagonals at the top of
each loop are extended
across the square to
interweave through the
top of the next loop in a
continuous motif.

135

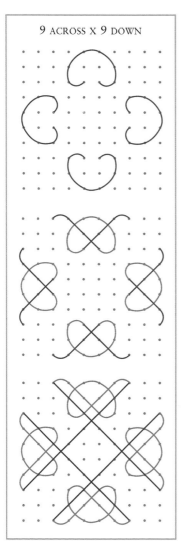

9 ACROSS X 9 DOWN

A variation of Design 119 in which the four loops are plotted facing each other in a square formation. The diagonals at the top of each loop are extended across the square to interweave through the top of the next loop into a continuous motif.

136

11 ACROSS X 11 DOWN

A variation of Designs 123 and 130, with angled corners.

COMBINATIONS & CORNERS

Combining different elements opens up design possibilities. Hearts can be combined with loops to add interest to a design and can also provide a decorative way of closing off or joining ribbons.

Motifs can be created specifically as corner designs by using the split ribbon technique, and mitred corners can be achieved by plotting panels at right angles to each other, and extending their free ends to make a decorative joint.

Chapter 11

Combined Hearts & Loops

The designs in this section are all plotted from hearts and loops, but patterns from other sections can also be combined to develop further knotwork ribbons.

137

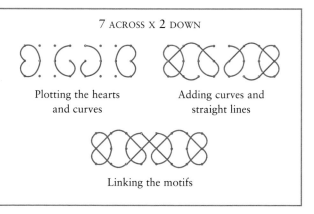

7 ACROSS X 2 DOWN

Plotting the hearts and curves

Adding curves and straight lines

Linking the motifs

A continuous border in which the loop design can be extended indefinitely and finished at either end with a heart.

138

8 ACROSS X 2 DOWN

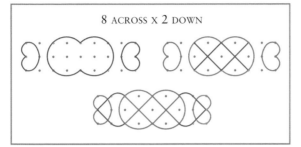

A motif of two interwoven hearts combined with a straight line design.

139

9 ACROSS X 2 DOWN

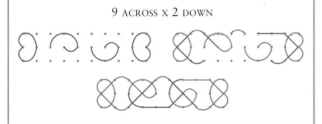

The loops are plotted one square apart and the ends are decorated with hearts to finish off this continuous border.

140

11 ACROSS X 2 DOWN

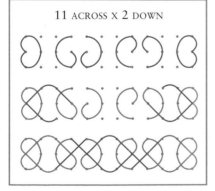

A variation of Design 137 in which pairs of small loops are plotted one square apart with loops alternately at the top and bottom. Again, the ends are decorated with small hearts.

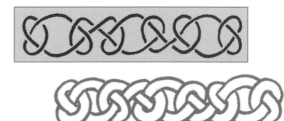

141

12 ACROSS X 3 DOWN

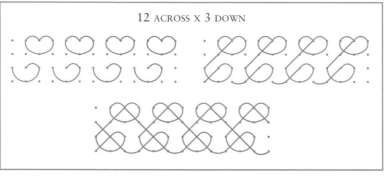

Two interwoven
ribbons of alternate
hearts and loops.

142

8 ACROSS X 4 DOWN

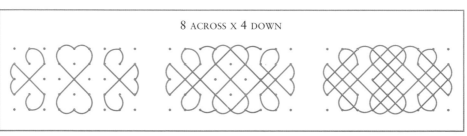

A continuous motif in which the heart bases are
extended and combined with loops.

143

16 ACROSS X 4 DOWN

Hearts plotted one square apart with diagonals extended over four squares. The design is three interwoven ribbons, each one making a repeated pattern of heart, small loop, heart.

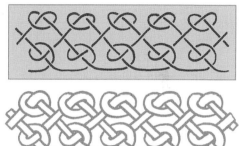

144

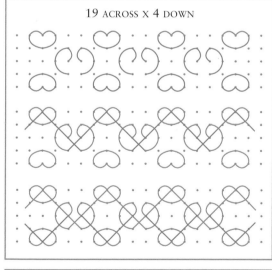

19 ACROSS X 4 DOWN

Two interwoven ribbons, similar to Design 143, in which the heart appears at both the top and bottom of the design, with the diagonals scribing a small loop.

145

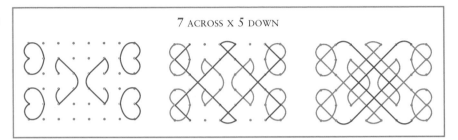

7 ACROSS X 5 DOWN

This design, which is a
continuous motif, uses the small
heart, extended loop and a twist
decoration at the top and bottom.

146

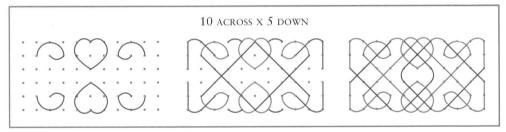

10 ACROSS X 5 DOWN

The small loop is
combined with the
large heart to give
a continuous motif.

147

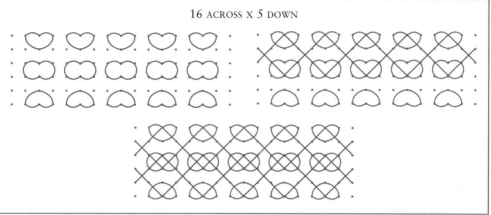

16 ACROSS X 5 DOWN

A variation of Design 138 in which individual motifs are woven into a border design.

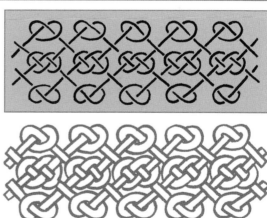

148

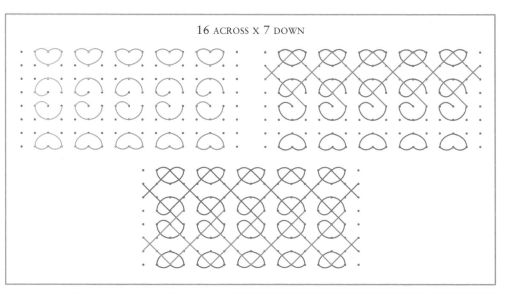

16 ACROSS X 7 DOWN

A variation of Design 144 in which the diagonals from the hearts are further extended. This allows two small loops to be inserted in the centre of the design. The ends of the border could be decorated with small hearts, drawn where the diagonals meet.

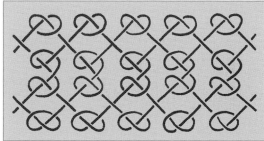

149

19 ACROSS X 7 DOWN

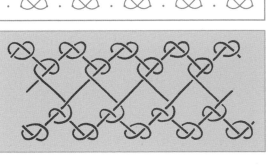

Another variation of Design
143 in which two small
loops are plotted into one
diagonal from each heart.
Three interwoven ribbons
make up this border.

150

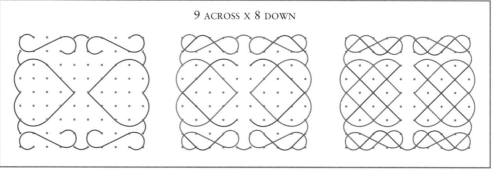

9 ACROSS X 8 DOWN

The large heart is drawn across four squares and the additional diagonals interweave with two small loops. The motif is continuous.

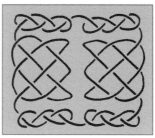

151

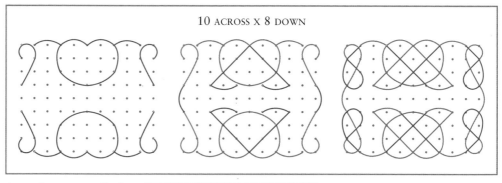

10 ACROSS X 8 DOWN

A continuous motif of large hearts and loops. Note that the loops in this design are extended over three squares.

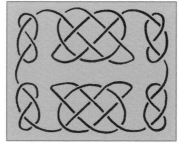

152

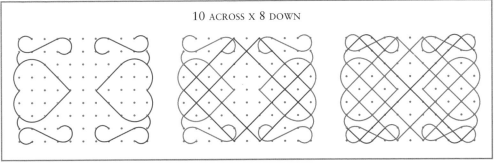

A variation of Design 150 in which the hearts are plotted two squares apart to allow the diagonals to extend across the centre of the design.

153

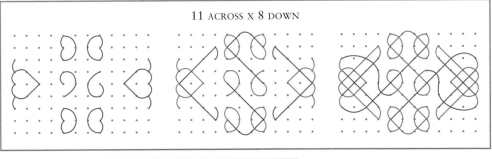

A continuous motif which demonstrates a method of breaking a border allowing extensions to either side.

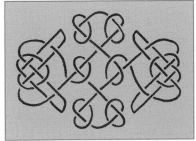

154

11 ACROSS X 8 DOWN

Two interwoven motifs combining large and small hearts with loops.

155

12 ACROSS X 9 DOWN

Base extensions of large hearts combine with loops to form a continuous motif.

Chapter 12

STRAIGHT LINES

◆

In the previous sections the hearts or loops have been plotted first and then joined by straight lines – all the designs in this section are constructed by plotting the straight lines first.

156

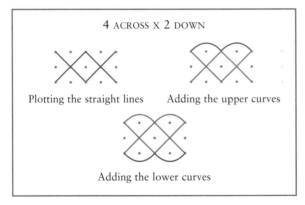

4 ACROSS X 2 DOWN

Plotting the straight lines   Adding the upper curves

Adding the lower curves

Lines drawn at 45° to the vertical and joined together at the top and bottom into a motif of two interwoven links.

157

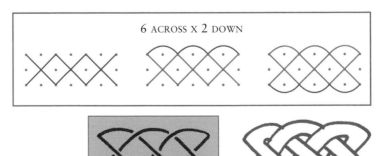

6 ACROSS X 2 DOWN

A variation of Design 156 in which a continuous motif is created by the addition of two further diagonals.

158

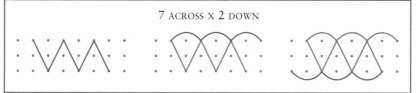

7 ACROSS X 2 DOWN

This simple double knot is plotted by drawing straight lines diagonally through two vertical squares. Note that the diagonals are not at 45° as they have been in all the previous designs.

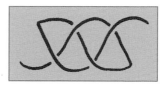

159

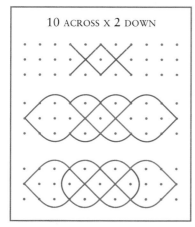

10 ACROSS X 2 DOWN

Two individual motifs which interweave.

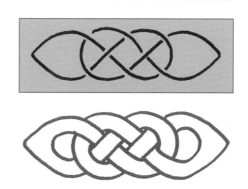

160

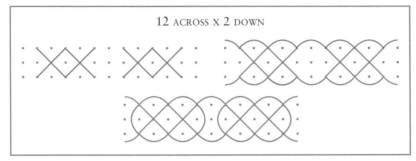

12 ACROSS X 2 DOWN

This design is an extension of Design 159 into a border in which individual motifs interweave.

161

13 ACROSS X 2 DOWN

An extension of Design 158 into a border design. This is an example of 'breaking' a plait. The result is a series of knots on a continuous ribbon.

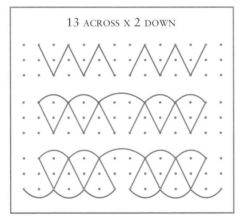

· STRAIGHT LINES ·

162

14 ACROSS X 2 DOWN

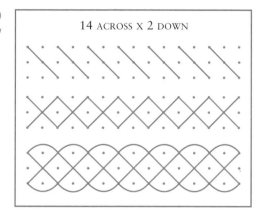

When straight lines are drawn at 45° to the vertical and joined at the top with curves, the result is a continuous ribbon which can be drawn to any length. Design 156, in which two individual links are formed, is an exception to this.

163

17 ACROSS X 2 DOWN

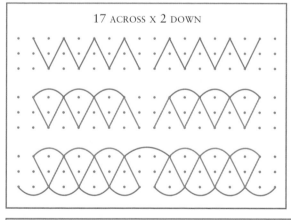

Continuous ribbons of any length can be drawn provided there is an odd number of 'diagonals' on either side of the break. The break is made by leaving one blank square between each group of diagonal lines.

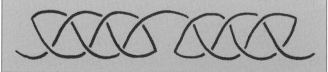

164

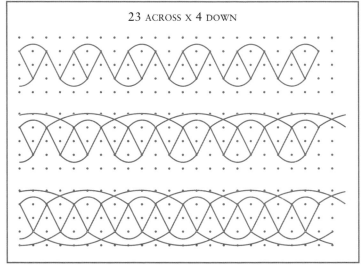

23 ACROSS X 4 DOWN

Lines are plotted diagonally across two vertical squares, but in this design there is no break in the lines. Instead, the break is made between the curves at the top and bottom of the lines. There are five interwoven ribbons in this border.

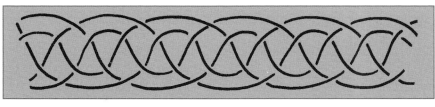

165

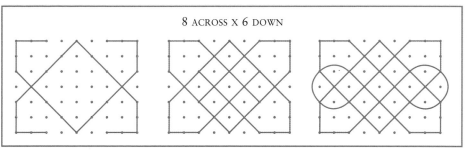

8 ACROSS X 6 DOWN

Plotted from straight
lines, this design is
decorated with a circle
at each side.

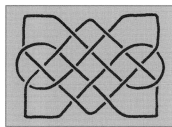

166

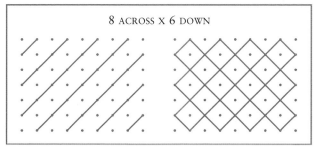

8 ACROSS X 6 DOWN

An example of classic plaiting, this is a continuous motif.

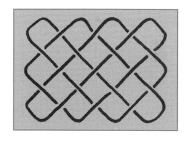

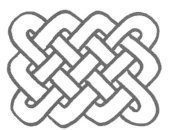

167

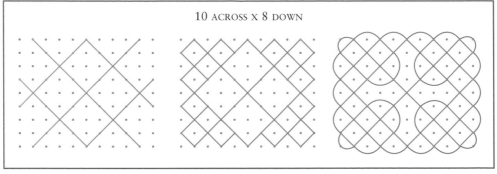

10 ACROSS X 8 DOWN

A further example of plaiting which clearly demonstrates the introduction of a 'break' in the centre of the design. The motif remains continuous as the original plaited design would have been.

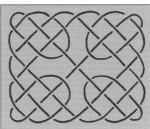

168

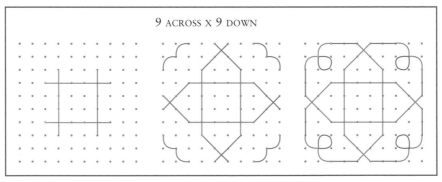

9 ACROSS X 9 DOWN

A tight motif of straight lines using twists to add decoration to the corners. The motif is continuous.

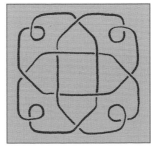

169

10 ACROSS X 8 DOWN

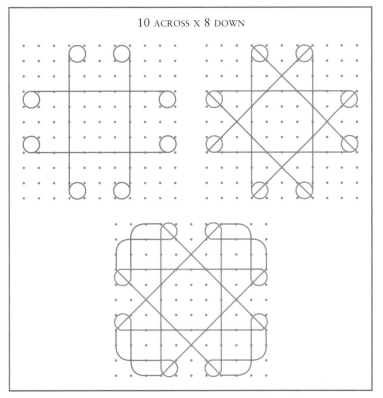

This continuous motif uses twists to fill in the corners.

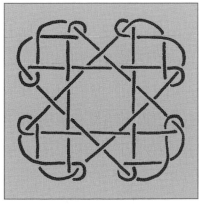

170

11 ACROSS X 11 DOWN

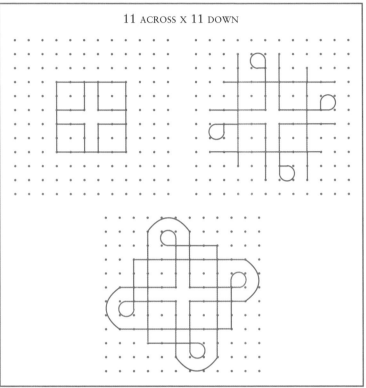

A continuous motif from *The Book of Durrow*.

171

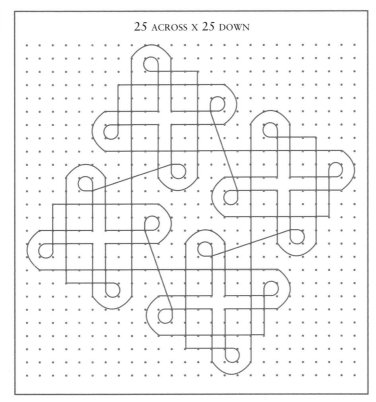

25 ACROSS X 25 DOWN

Design 170 arranged as a panel. This can be extended to cover any area and if the grid is plotted diagonally, the knotwork will be rotated through 45°.

Chapter 13

CORNER MOTIFS

Many small motifs have been included in the previous chapters for purely decorative purposes. Motifs can also be created specifically for corner designs. The split ribbon technique is very useful for this as it enables knotwork patterns to be contained within a border frame, with the whole making up one complete, single unit.

All the motifs shown here are plotted using a base from the previous chapters.

172

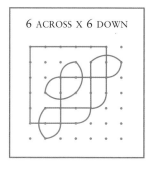

6 ACROSS X 6 DOWN

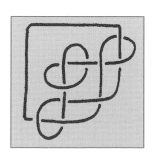

Small heart with diagonal twist.

173

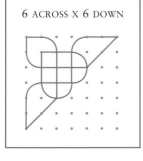

6 ACROSS X 6 DOWN

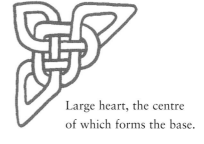

Large heart, the centre
of which forms the base.

174

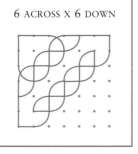

6 ACROSS X 6 DOWN

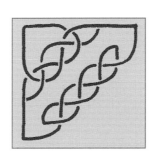

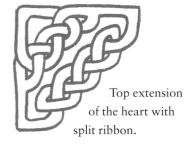

Top extension
of the heart with
split ribbon.

175

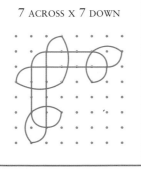

7 ACROSS X 7 DOWN

An extended loop forms the corner with two hearts
extended from the diagonals.

176

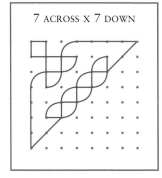

7 ACROSS X 7 DOWN

A heart with a twisted base forms the corner and two hearts with top extensions are plotted across the diagonal.

177

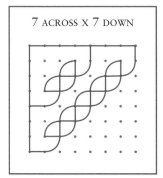

7 ACROSS X 7 DOWN

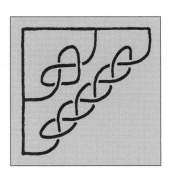

Three hearts plotted with top and base extensions.

178

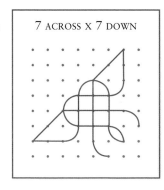

7 ACROSS X 7 DOWN

A large heart with decoration at the base.

179

8 ACROSS X 8 DOWN

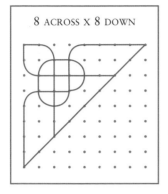

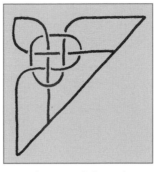

Large heart with base decoration and split ribbons across the diagonal.

180

8 ACROSS X 8 DOWN

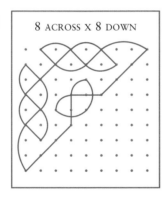

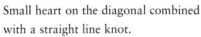

Small heart on the diagonal combined with a straight line knot.

181

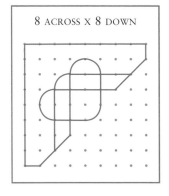

8 ACROSS X 8 DOWN

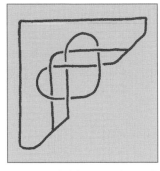

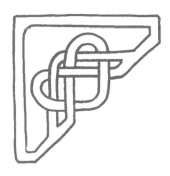

An extended loop with a split ribbon on the diagonal.

182

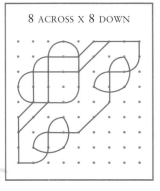

8 ACROSS X 8 DOWN

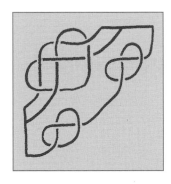

A variation of Design 181 in which the extended loop forms the corner and two small hearts decorate the diagonal.

183

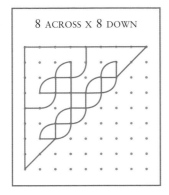

8 ACROSS X 8 DOWN

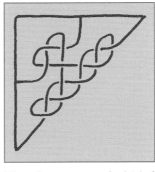

Three hearts, two of which form the diagonal with top extensions.

184

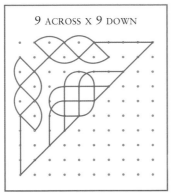

9 ACROSS X 9 DOWN

A large heart plotted across the diagonal with straight line knots forming the corners. The ribbon is split three times on the diagonal.

185

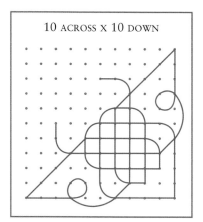

10 ACROSS X 10 DOWN

A design based on original plaitwork, i.e. straight lines.

186

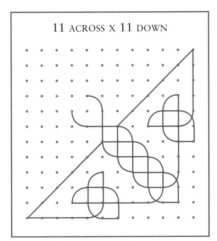

11 ACROSS X 11 DOWN

The centre is two hearts with top and base extensions. Additional decoration uses small hearts with base extensions.

Chapter 14

MITRED CORNERS

◆

Continuous borders and panels can be adapted to produce decorative frames by joining two lengths at a mitred corner. There are various ways of creating mitred corners – it is simply a matter of finding a way to turn the free ends of the ribbons through 45°.

A useful method of working this out is to draw a length of the border or panel on graph paper and then cut a section out. When the cut-out section is placed at 90° to the remaining length of border, a suitable way of joining the ribbons can be found. (See Chapter 2, Materials and Techniques, page 15; see also Fig 2.23.)

The corners presented here have been developed from designs appearing in the earlier chapters, for which step-by-step plottings and crossing points have been given.

187

7 ACROSS X 1 DOWN

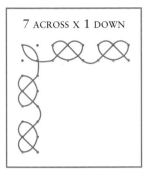

Developed from Design 1
(see Small Hearts, page 22).

188

12 ACROSS X 1 DOWN

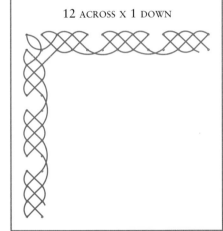

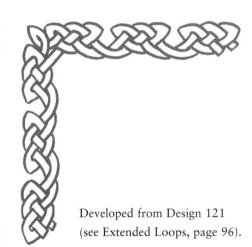

Developed from Design 121
(see Extended Loops, page 96).

189

7 ACROSS X 2 DOWN

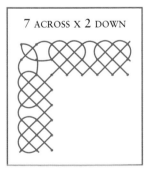

189 Developed from Design 24
(see Large Hearts, page 37).

190

7 ACROSS X 2 DOWN

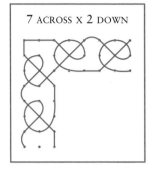

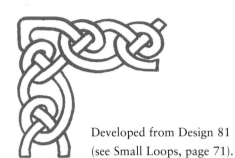

Developed from Design 81
(see Small Loops, page 71).

191

8 ACROSS X 2 DOWN

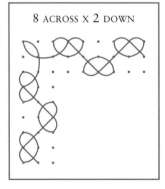

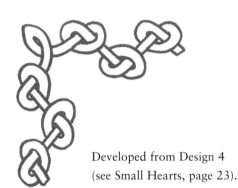

Developed from Design 4
(see Small Hearts, page 23).

192

8 ACROSS X 2 DOWN

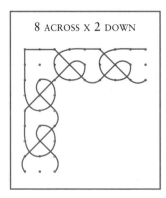

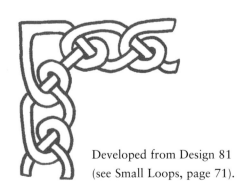

Developed from Design 81
(see Small Loops, page 71).

193

9 ACROSS X 2 DOWN

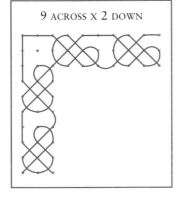

Developed from Design 84
(see Small Loops, page 72).

194

9 ACROSS X 2 DOWN

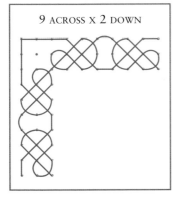

Developed from Design 84
(see Small Loops, page 72).

195

9 ACROSS X 2 DOWN

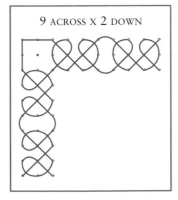

Developed from Design 80
(see Small Loops, page 71).

196

9 ACROSS X 2 DOWN

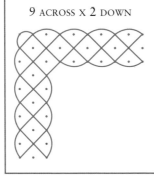

Developed from Design 162
(see Straight Lines, page 123).

197

11 ACROSS X 2 DOWN

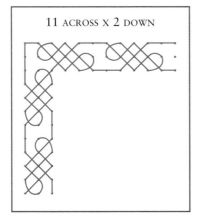

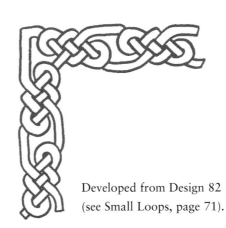

Developed from Design 82
(see Small Loops, page 71).

198

11 ACROSS X 2 DOWN

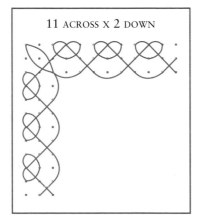

Developed from Design 3
(see Small Hearts, page 23).

199

14 ACROSS X 2 DOWN

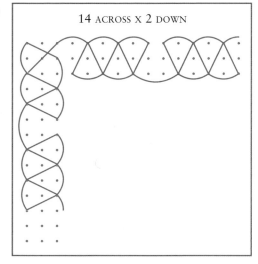

Developed from Design 161
(see Straight Lines, page 122).

200

12 ACROSS X 3 DOWN

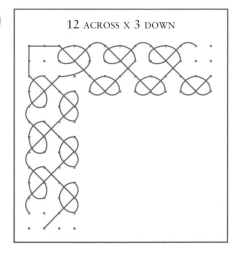

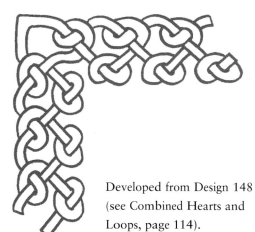

Developed from Design 148
(see Combined Hearts and
Loops, page 114).

201

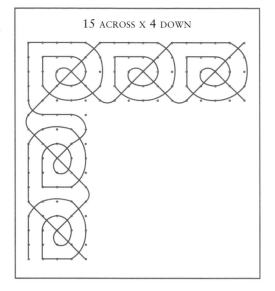

15 ACROSS X 4 DOWN

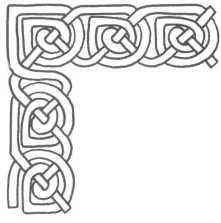

Developed from Design 108
(see Large Loops, page 88).

202

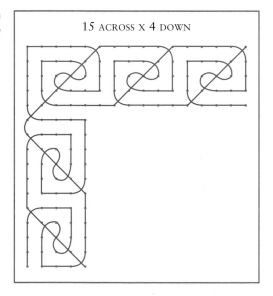

15 ACROSS X 4 DOWN

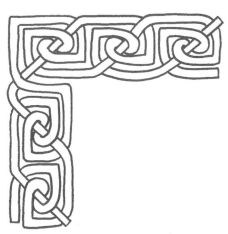

Developed from Design 110
(see Large Loops, page 89).

203

22 ACROSS X 6 DOWN

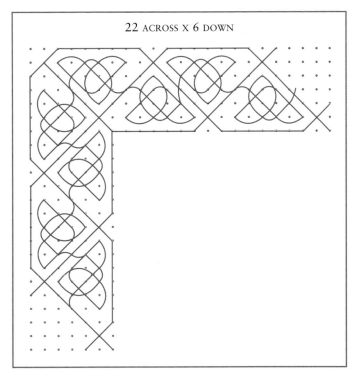

Developed from Design 132
(see Extended Loops, page 102).

Introduction to Zoomorphics

Zoomorphic designs include animal, reptile, fish or bird motifs. Human figures are known as anthropomorphics. Heads and tails can be added to finish off the ends of knotwork borders or inserted into a point where the ribbon is not interwoven. More intricate lacing can be achieved by extending feet, eyes, ears, tails and tongues to produce further knotting. Bands of animals can be joined by allowing each creature to bite the one in front.

There are many designs composed entirely of animals, wonderful examples being the four gospels in *The Book of Kells* in which Matthew is depicted as a lion, Mark as a man (or angel), Luke as a calf, and John as an eagle.

The motifs presented here have been developed from designs appearing in the earlier chapters, for which step-by-step plottings and crossing points have been given. The designs should be plotted and completed in the usual way. The next step is where the true artistic touch shows! There are no rules when filling in the bodies of animals and the leaves of plants – imagination must run freely.

Chapter 15

fish

---◆---

The fish is the symbol of Christianity and has been a symbol of Christ since the second century AD. The fish is common in *The Book of Kells*, accompanying the face or name of Christ.

Additional embellishment can be taken from the eyes, mouth, tail and fins of fish motifs, and colour and decoration used to fill in fins and scales.

A combination of materials and quilling
techniques can be used to good effect.

204

13 ACROSS x 2 DOWN

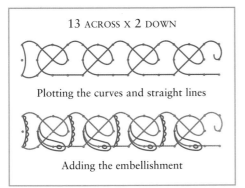

Plotting the curves and straight lines

Adding the embellishment

Based on a small loop, the addition of heads and tails produces a continuous border. Developed from Design 81 (see Small Loops, page 71).

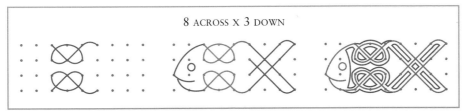

205

8 ACROSS x 3 DOWN

Two small hearts embellished to produce an elongated fish. Developed from Design 5 (see Small Hearts, page 24).

206

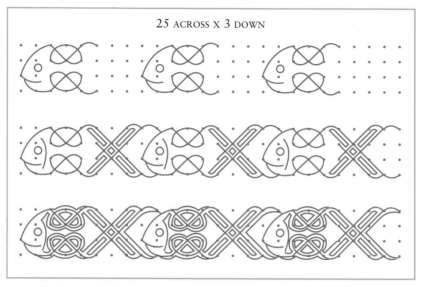

25 ACROSS X 3 DOWN

A border design developed from Design 5 (see Small Hearts, page 24), by extending lines from the mouth and head.

207

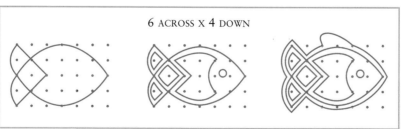

6 ACROSS X 4 DOWN

A small heart with a right-angled base developed into a motif.

208

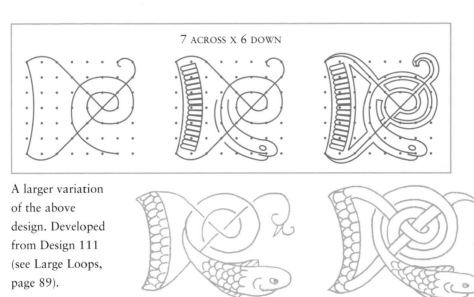

7 ACROSS X 6 DOWN

A larger variation of the above design. Developed from Design 111 (see Large Loops, page 89).

Chapter 16

Snakes

◆

The snake has dual imagery. It was a symbol of Christ's resurrection due to the belief that its skin shedding was a renewal of youth, however, it was also associated with the fall of man.

For snake motifs, lines can be extended from the eyes and tail.

209

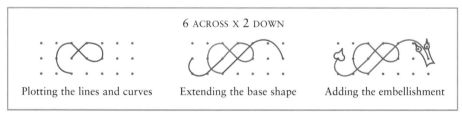

6 ACROSS X 2 DOWN

| Plotting the lines and curves | Extending the base shape | Adding the embellishment |

A simple snake based on a small loop. Developed from Design 84 (see Small Loops, page 72).

210

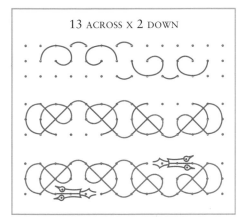

13 ACROSS X 2 DOWN

Interest has been added to the border by using a long loop as the head and tail of a snake. Developed from a base of small loops.

211

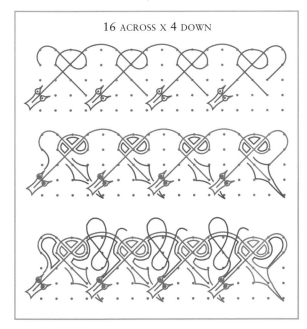

16 ACROSS X 4 DOWN

A loop is divided into the head and tail of a snake. Developed from Design 81 (see Small Loops, page 71).

212

9 ACROSS X 9 DOWN

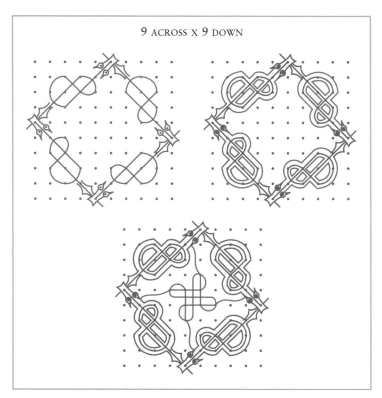

If the centre is left unfilled, this design can be used as a border by extending the corners into longer lines to frame the design. Alternatively, the centre can be filled with additional knotwork, as shown here. Developed from Designs 89 and 98 (see Small Loops, pages 75 and 81).

213

10 ACROSS X 10 DOWN

A larger design of two interwoven snakes. Additional ribbons which interweave with the large ribbons have been taken from the eyes.

Chapter 17

Dogs

◆

For the Celts, dogs were symbolic of hunting, healing and
health. They were also associated with the role of protector:
the Dutch goddess, Nehalennia, is often depicted with a dog
that is clearly acting as her protector.

Designs can be added to or embellished by taking extensions
from the ears and tongue.

214

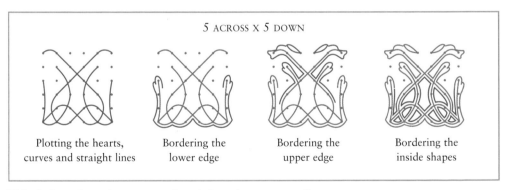

5 ACROSS X 5 DOWN

| Plotting the hearts, curves and straight lines | Bordering the lower edge | Bordering the upper edge | Bordering the inside shapes |

This design of two interwoven dogs is based on two small
hearts plotted together as a top extension. The diagonals of
each heart are extended to form the head and front leg of each
dog, and the hind leg is taken from the outside top edge of the
heart. I bordered the edge before the inside shapes on this
design to make it easier to see the construction of the dog.

215

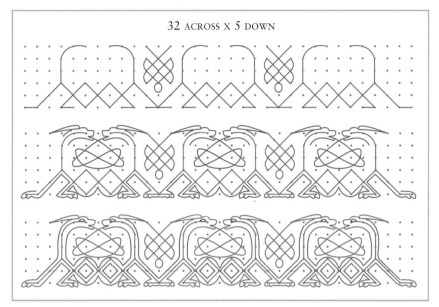

32 ACROSS X 5 DOWN

A border of interwoven dogs in which the spaces have been used for additional embellishment. Developed from Designs 39, 117 and 156 (see Extending the Base, Extended Loops and Straight Lines, pages 46, 94 and 120).

216

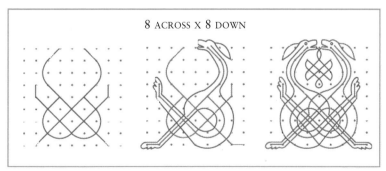

8 ACROSS X 8 DOWN

Similar to Design 214, this design is based on the large heart (see Chapter 4). Note that the pointed heart top is not used in the motif.

Chapter 18

BIRDS

---- ◆ ----

In Christian art, the peacock symbolized the incorruptibility of Christ. This had its roots in an ancient belief that the flesh of the peacock was so hard that it would not putrefy. The eagle is an important Celtic symbol. During the Romano-Celtic period, the myths surrounding the Celtic sun god merged with those of the Roman god, Jupiter, who was represented by an eagle, and the eagle came to be a sacred Celtic symbol.

Additional embellishment can be added to bird motifs by extending lines from the neck, feet and tail feathers.

217

17 ACROSS X 6 DOWN

Plotting the straight lines and adding bird heads

Adding large hearts

Bordering the inside shapes and adding
tails and feet

Bird motif using a large heart,
and interweaving four necks.

218

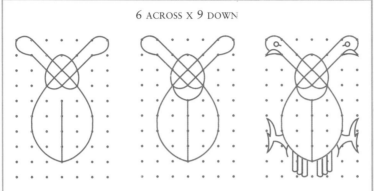

6 ACROSS X 9 DOWN

A variation of Design 217, using a
large heart to interweave the necks.

The border design on this plate is
echoed in the central motif.

219

2 ACROSS X 31 DOWN

A border of interwoven birds, developed
from Design 84 (see Small Loops, page 72).

220

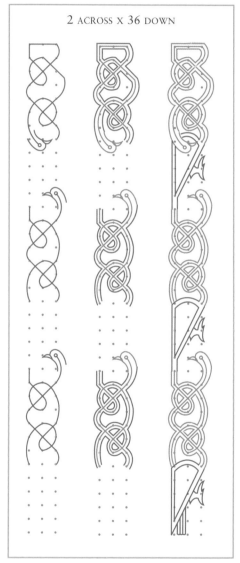

2 ACROSS X 36 DOWN

Loose ends of ribbons are 'closed off' with bird heads in this border. In the ribbon-work, lines are extended from the feet so that each bird 'bites' the one in front.

221

2 ACROSS X 41 DOWN

A border of interwoven birds, developed
from Design 162 (see Straight Lines, page 123).

Chapter 19

PLANTS

◆

Plant motifs, depicted in *The Book of Kells* and on many Irish crosses, can be attributed to the vine, a symbol of Christ, and the tree of life is a well-known Celtic symbol. Trees also reflect the joining of the lower and upper worlds, with the roots reaching down into the earth and the branches reaching up to the sky.

222

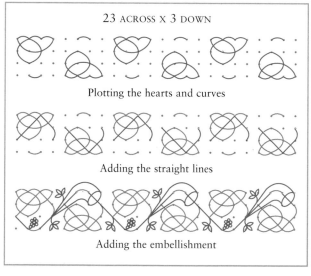

23 ACROSS x 3 DOWN

Plotting the hearts and curves

Adding the straight lines

Adding the embellishment

The long loops on one side of the design have been extended into cornucopia and leaves have been added to the loose ends of ribbons. The ribbon-work shows a variation, developed from the same starting point. Developed from Design 132 (see Extended Loops, page 102).

· P L A N T S ·

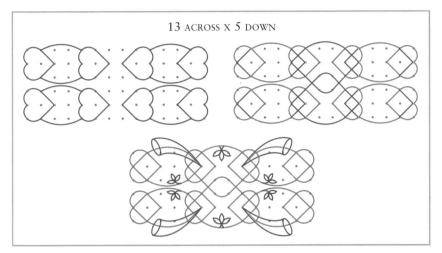

223

13 ACROSS X 5 DOWN

This design can be varied by joining the hearts, using a top extension, and interweaving the long loops. Developed from Design 52 (see Extending the Top, page 54).

224

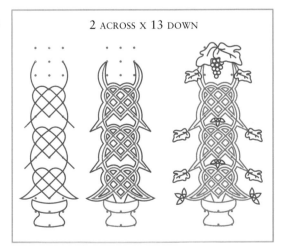

2 ACROSS X 13 DOWN

Diagonals extended from the top of the heart have been embellished with leaves. Developed from Design 52 (see Extending the Top, page 54).

PART THREE

Adaptations & Decorations

Chapter 20

CREATING YOUR OWN DESIGNS

◆

Excellent knotwork can be achieved by tracing or copying designs, but creating your own gives you the freedom to combine, adapt and plot designs to suit exact requirements.

The initial difficulty when attempting knotwork is understanding how the ribbons interweave, but confidence is gained with practice. The method in this book is reliable and simple and can be applied to any knotwork design.

Once the principles of this method are understood, you can experiment with plotting shapes in different positions and trying alternative ways of extending, embellishing and joining them.

Try drawing hearts or loops over a sheet of paper and joining them in different ways by extending lines from each. Varying the placement of the hearts and loops will produce different designs, and modifying their basic shape will open up the possibilities still more.

Grids

The designs in Part 2 were all plotted on a regular grid, but even this can be modified, and as the grid influences the outline of the final design, this gives you the freedom to fill all kinds of shapes.

Throughout the book the designs have been plotted on square or rectangular grids, and these grids have been measured in terms of the number of squares across and the number of squares down. When grids are modified to fit other shapes, these 'squares' become distorted so that they are no longer true squares. To avoid confusion, the 'squares' in modified grids are referred to as divisions.

Circular and other geometric designs

As for squares and rectangles, the space to be filled must be marked into the number of divisions required to fit the chosen design. However, with circular grids these divisions will not be squares, and will not be of a uniform size: they become narrower as they move towards the centre of the circle and wider as they move away from it.

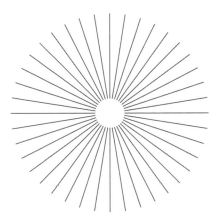

FIG 20.1 Marking out the divisions 'across' for a circular design.

Translating the design to a circular grid, the number of divisions across equates with the number of divisions around the circumference of the circle, and these are marked out using a protractor. For example, a design that fills four divisions across will require a total number of divisions that is divisible by four. If nine repeats of the design are desired, 36 divisions will be required. The angle at which to mark out each division is found by dividing the circumference of the circle, 360°, by the number of divisions there will be. In this example the angle required is 10° (360° ÷ 36), so lines extending out from

a central point are drawn at angles of 10° from each other. (See Fig 20.1.)

The number of divisions down is marked out by scribing concentric and equidistant circles over these lines. The number of circles that need to be scribed is one more than the number of divisions required. In Fig 20.2, two divisions down are required so three concentric circles have been scribed.

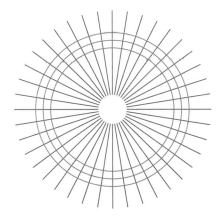

FIG 20.2 Equidistant circles are scribed to mark the divisions 'down'.

The actual size of each division, and thus of the motifs in the design, is determined by the radii of the circles scribed (the bigger the radius, the bigger the design), so these should be set accordingly. When a pattern with several divisions is selected, the centre row will be the closest to regular squares – those above will be wider and those below narrower.

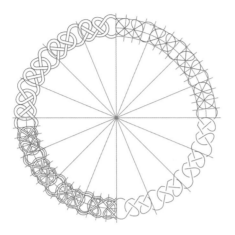

FIG 20.3 Various stages in the completion of a circular design.

The same method is used for drafting designs to fit other geometric shapes, such as hexagons and pentagons, adjusting the 'circumference' to fit the outline of the particular shape.

Irregular shapes

Grids can be adapted to fill any size or shape. It is not really necessary to have a grid, but it does help if the irregular shape is to be mirrored in a different part of the design, for example, in each corner. Irregular grids are simple to con-

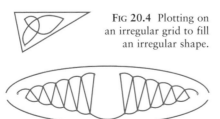

FIG 20.4 Plotting on an irregular grid to fill an irregular shape.

struct. Divisions are used as for a regular grid and marked over the shape, across and down, but are drawn to conform to the shape. This means that the grid produced is not composed of regular, square divisions and the knots produced will not be uniform (see Fig 20.4). A typical example is a small heart which has half of its top extended over two or more divisions.

Substituting an outline with a knot

To substitute a knot for an outline, trace the outline of the shape and select or create a knot. The design used for the fish

FIG 20.5 A knot is substituted for the outline, but the original fin is retained.

in Figs 20.5–20.7 was Design 205 (see Fish, page 149). Mark a grid within the outline – this may be regular or irregular as required – and plot the design in the usual way. The whole outline can be included in the knot, or some parts kept as for the original design.

The examples of fish, shown here, demonstrate the method. The knot in

FIG 20.6 The same design as Fig 20.5, but with the fin included as part of the knot.

Fig 20.5 shows the fins kept as part of the original outline, while the knots in Figs 20.6 and 20.7 show the fin included as part of the ribbon. This is done following the zoomorphic method of extending ribbons to form limbs, tongues and tails. (See pages 147–151.)

Embellishment

For a more decorative border or motif, two or more knots may be combined in the one design. For a lighter touch, and to avoid overcrowding, one of these knots could be left as line work rather than being converted into ribbons as has been done in Designs 212 and 215 (see pages 154 and 157).

Free ends of ribbons can be extended and closed off with zoomorphic motifs or with a simple node (see Design 208, page 151). Ribbons can also be looped, twisted and curled (see Fig 20.8).

FIG 20.7 An embellished motif of two fish, with knots substituted for their outlines.

Use a small or large heart to embellish the joining point of two ribbons

Cross the ends of the ribbons to form a small or large twist

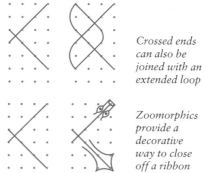

Crossed ends can also be joined with an extended loop

Zoomorphics provide a decorative way to close off a ribbon

FIG 20.8 Alternative methods of closing ribbons.

Chapter 21

Using Knotwork Designs in Other Crafts

FIG 21.1 An example of needlepoint lace showing how the cordonnet emphasizes the outline of a knot.

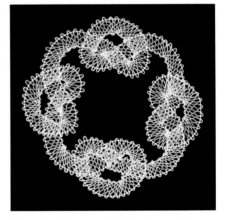

FIG 21.2 A knotwork design created in bobbin lace.

Lace

True lace has been made since the early-sixteenth century. The two main types of handmade lace are needlepoint and bobbin lace.

Needlepoint, or point lace, is made, as the name suggests, using a needle. The stitch used is buttonhole stitch. The pattern is defined with a cordonnet (outline) of thick cotton.

Bobbin lace, also known as pillow lace, is made using threads wound round a bobbin. The challenge in creating a knotwork design in bobbin lace is

FIG 21.3 A knot has been substituted for the outline of the fish in this example of carrickmacross.

to keep the lacework as one continuous piece, with no sewing in the lace.

Needlepoint lace tends to be stiffer than bobbin lace.

Carrickmacross

Carrickmacross needlepoint lace, reverse appliqué, originated in the town of Carrickmacross in Ireland in the nineteenth century, and is characterized by picots and pops. Traditionally, it consists of white cotton organdie which is attached to fine white cotton net by oversewing a pattern in white cotton. However, bright colours were used in the sample above, in keeping with Celtic design.

Calligraphy

The word 'calligraphy' is derived from the Greek words 'kalle' and 'graphe',

FIG 21.4 An original knotwork design for the letter 'I'.

FIG 21.5 This lively design uses the bright colours characteristic of Celtic art.

and means beautiful writing. Writing is a form of drawing, and the twenty-six 'symbols' that make up the English alphabet can be arranged in many different ways, with composition and shape playing a major role.

FIG 21.6 The outline of small dots on this design is a feature used throughout *The Lindisfarne Gospels*.

China painting

Knotwork designs can be used just as they are for painting onto china, though it can be more difficult to produce the fine lines with a brush as accurately as can be done with a pen or pencil.

Never use china in which there are cracks as they will cause the china to break during firing.

Quilling

The art of quilling, or paper filigree, was probably inspired by metal filigree where gold and silver wires were used to create intricate and delicate designs. Quilling is thought to have originated over five hundred years ago, but little of its history is recorded and the quillwork preserved in museums dates from the late-eighteenth or early-nineteenth centuries, when paper became less

FIG 21.7 The use of different materials and quilling techniques adds textural interest to this design.

costly and was, therefore, more readily available.

It is not easy to make quilling precise, and illustrating knotwork using quilling techniques presents several problems. The first is obtaining the very fine outlines that are central to knotwork. In the design shown above, tight circles of black quilling paper were glued in an upright position all around the outer and inner lines. The second problem is maintaining the symmetry that is integral to so many knotwork designs. This, combined with the clearly defined spaces to be filled, limits the number of quilling techniques that can be employed, but colour and other materials, such as beads, shells and pressed flowers, can be used to compensate.

Counted thread work

The many techniques of counted thread work include the three shown here – cross stitch, Assisi work and beadwork on canvas.

FIG 21.8 Curved lines and rounded corners need to be squared-off to make them suitable for a cross stitch design.

FIG 21.9 The characteristic outlining of the main design in Assisi work emphasizes the interweaving of knotwork patterns.

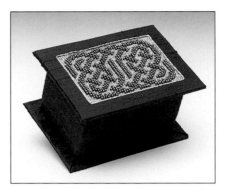

FIG 21.10 To create the impression of interweaving in beadwork, small areas of the design, where the lines cross, are left unworked.

Counted thread work is applied to fabrics woven with the same number of threads per inch in both warp and weft. Each stitch or bead is worked over a regular number of threads, covering a small square of fabric. Patterns are usually worked out on graph paper, with each square of the paper representing one stitch. The effect is quite stylized, especially in the case of small motifs, as the curved lines must be adapted to conform to the straight lines of graph paper and fabric threads (see Adapting Curves and Rounded Corners, page 178).

Embroidery

Embroidery has a long and distinguished history. There are references to embroidery in the writings of Homer and examples of embroidered roundels dating from around the fourth century.

FIG 21.11 Embroidery is an example of needlework where the curved lines of knotwork can be directly followed.

FIG 21.12 The two ribbons in this design are indicated through the use of different materials.

In China, it is thought that embroidery was an established craft by 2000 BC.

Freehand embroidery is well suited to knotwork designs as it requires little adaptation from the original design: once the pattern is drafted, it can be transferred straight to the background fabric.

Patchwork

Early patchwork was purely utilitarian, with scraps of old, worn fabrics being stitched together to make 'new' clothes and bed coverings. It was not until materials became cheaper and more readily available, and there was more free time for such things, that the decorative possibilities of patchwork could be explored. By the late-eighteenth century patchwork was being used decoratively.

Incorporating knotwork in a patchwork design is quite a straightforward process – the knot to be followed can be simply transferred to the background material. What was essential in the example shown left, was the use of bias pressing bar in the material used to form the outlining: this eased the interweaving of the strips of material, and enabled them to be stretched around the curves and mitred at the corners.

Embossing

Embossed cards are produced by pressing card or paper into a cut-out design so that the impression of the design is left in low relief on the card. Good quality thick paper or card should be used. Textured watercolour paper gives a pleasant effect and it is worth experimenting with coloured card, though white is best for enhancing the shadows. Most knotwork designs can be adapted

FIG 21.13 A collection of embossed knotwork designs.

for embossing quite easily by breaking ribbons where they pass underneath another ribbon, and then 'sealing' the open ends.

Parchment craft

Embossing and perforating are used in parchment craft to create delicate raised designs on artificial parchment paper. Parchment craft is thought to have been used in the Spanish cloisters in the

FIG 21.14 The embossed areas on artificial parchment show up whiter than the surrounding paper.

FIG 21.15 The dark background material in this paperweight shows up the perforations in the design more clearly.

fifteenth century and to have been introduced from there to the Spanish colonies in South America. The craft has since been brought back to Europe and is enjoying increasing popularity.

Knotwork designs are well suited for use in parchment craft: the knotwork design is traced lightly onto the paper with a mapping pen, the only adaptation required being to break lines where they pass under other lines.

Pyrography

Pyrography, burnt-wood etching, and poker work are all names by which the art of burning designs onto materials is known. The term pyrography was coined by the Victorians from the Greek words 'pûr', meaning fire, and 'graphos', meaning writing. The craft has been practised all over the world in

FIG 21.16 The pyrograph can be used to produce very effective shading.

one form or another, almost certainly since the discovery of fire. Pyrographed knotwork designs are very effective and are relatively easy to achieve. The chosen design can be traced onto the wood, or other material, in pencil, and this outline then traced over with the heated poker.

Woodcarving

The range of woodcarving tools is ever-increasing, but it is possible to carve using only a few simple tools – whittling requires only a sharp knife – and woodcarving has been used to make both practical and decorative pieces since

FIG 21.17   To give the impression of interweaving, ribbons passing under another ribbon are graded down a little at either side of the crossing point.

man fashioned the first sharp tools. Knotwork designs can be drawn directly onto the wood or plotted on paper and then traced. Irregular designs will often be required to fit the available spaces on furniture and other pieces: these can be worked out on adapted grids beforehand.

For the design shown in Fig 21.17, the outlines of the knots were defined first by carving away a portion of the wood, then the internal shapes were removed. To create the impression of interweaving, the ribbons were graded down a little on either side of the ribbon under which they passed.

Adapting curves and rounded corners

There are some crafts, popular examples including knitting and cross stitch, in

FIG 21.18 Squaring off gives this familiar heart design a new look.

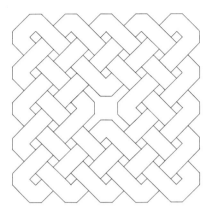

FIG 21.19 Straight lines and sharp corners produce a very strong design.

FIG 21.21 A series of border patterns have been used to build up the overall design for this tam-o'-shanter.

which the curves of Celtic knotwork cannot be followed, and for these all the curves must be 'squared off'. A simple way to square off a design is to plot it, in pencil, with the curves, and then draw in angles and straight lines to replace the curves. Go over the design with

FIG 21.20 The stone cross at St Molluag's, and a knitted representation.

the angles and straight lines in ink and then rub out the pencilled curves. The resulting pattern can then be transferred to the working piece as required. Examples of squared-off charts are given in Figs 21.18 and 21.19.

The knitted samples on this page show how effective squared-off designs can be. The wall hanging (see Fig 21.20) is based on the reconstructed cross at St Molluag's Church in Ness on the Isle of Lewis, and has a background that reflects the wild flowers that grow on the west coast of the Outer Hebrides. The knitting mixes traditional Fair Isle design with intarsia.

The tam-o'-shanter (see Fig 21.21) illustrates the adaptation of Celtic borders for knitting. Border patterns can be used in a similar way in sweaters, and interconnected border designs can be linked to form all-over patterns.

Chapter 22

Colour & Pattern in Knotwork

The colours traditionally used in knotwork were very bright. The best references to the colours used are the books of *Kells* and *Durrow* and *The Lindisfarne Gospels*: there are texts on the books of Kells and Lindisfarne with full-page, colour illustrations. For your own designs, the use of colour and pattern is a matter of personal choice. Here are just a few ideas.

Backgrounds

A bold effect is created when the background is blackened and the design left uncoloured. Alternatively, the background may be shaded or marbled in

black or grey. Another possibility is to fill in the background with various colours to resemble stained glass.

Stoning and graining are decorative techniques that can be used to great effect. Stoning is achieved by completely

FIG 22.2 A background decorated by stoning.

FIG 22.1 A blackened background against an uncoloured ribbon gives a bold effect.

FIG 22.3 An example of graining.

FIG 22.4 Outlining a design with small circles.

FIG 22.5 A background of scales: textured backgrounds
can be left black-and-white or coloured.

filling in the background with small dots (rather like sand), and graining by 'taking a line for a walk'. Graining will produce an indeterminate pattern, as shown in Fig 22.3.

A favourite method of decoration in *The Lindisfarne Gospels* was to outline a knot with a series of very small dots (see Fig 21.6 on page 174). Small circles can also be used in this way, or to fill in backgrounds, as can a pattern of scales (see Figs 22.4 and 22.5). These can all be left black-and-white, or shaded over with colour.

Ribbons

There is much that can be done to make a feature of the ribbon. You may choose

FIG 22.6 A simple design with each ribbon finished in a different colour.

to colour all the ribbons the same, or to highlight each strand with a different colour. The stained glass effect mentioned for backgrounds can also be applied to the ribbons, with a number of colours used on the one strand.

181

FIG 22.7 Shading ribbons at crossing points highlights the interweaving.

FIG 22.8 The ribbons are decorated with a coloured stripe down either side.

FIG 22.9 A different colour is used
for the stripe on each ribbon.

FIG 22.10 A single stripe down the
centre of each ribbon provides the
decoration for this design.

FIG 22.11
Corners are
decorated with
circles.

Shading ribbons can give a three-dimensional feel, and there are two main approaches to this: shading across the width of the ribbon, and shading at crossing points.

A common feature of Celtic designs is to use one main colour for a ribbon, and then use others in a stripe along their length, down the sides or down the centre. (See Figs 22.8–22.10.)

Decoration on ribbons may be in colour or in black. Coloured circles are a common element and are seen both along the length of ribbons, or in the corners only. A broken line can be scribed along the centre of a ribbon, or lines drawn at intervals across its width. Scales and feathers are appropriate for zoomorphic designs, and highlighting each with a different colour will make the pattern stand out.

FIG 22.12 Circles are used along the entire length of the ribbon.

FIG 22.13 A feather pattern decorates the wings on this bird motif.

General colouring tips

1 Try out various colour combinations before embarking on the actual ribbonwork. A small heart is useful fortesting colours. It is very quickly worked and has three points of interweaving which will show up different effects.

2 Try unlikely colours together for a dramatic effect.

3 Do not use colours which are very close in shade, as one tends to kill the other.

4 Be careful with dark colours and try them out first; they sometimes hide the knot and obscure the crossing points. For this reason dark colours are better with a light border on both sides of the ribbon.

5 Note carefully how many ribbons are interwoven in the selected design and work on one ribbon at a time – it is very frustrating when you find that you have coloured part of a different ribbon by mistake!

About the Author

Brought up during the war when few toys were available, Sheila was kept entertained with paper. Her father encouraged her to draw intricate patterns and make paper toys, and introduced her to the basic principles of paper engineering – a pastime which has become a lifetime pleasure.

She gives regular workshops in paper-related crafts for the County and Borough Councils, and in 1989 she was a runner-up in the BBC 2 Paper Engineering Competition.

Sheila is interested in many crafts. She enjoys designing and making automata, moving toys and tatting shuttles. Her collection of corn dollies and straw work is now on permanent display at Shugborough Hall.

Her other interests include golf and playing the clarinet with a local concert band. She is a Parish Council Clerk, qualified music teacher and, together with a friend, runs a book-keeping service for local traders.

Sheila lives in Lancashire with her husband and has three sons.

Celtic knot with a modern theme, drawn by one of Jack Dowling's primary school students.

GMC PUBLICATIONS

BOOKS

WOODTURNING

Adventures in Woodturning	*David Springett*	Practical Tips for Turners & Carvers	*GMC Publications*
Bert Marsh: Woodturner	*Bert Marsh*	Practical Tips for Woodturners	*GMC Publications*
Bill Jones' Notes from the Turning Shop	*Bill Jones*	Spindle Turning	*GMC Publications*
Bill Jones' Further Notes from the Turning Shop	*Bill Jones*	Turning Miniatures in Wood	*John Sainsbury*
Carving on Turning	*Chris Pye*	Turning Wooden Toys	*Terry Lawrence*
Colouring Techniques for Woodturners	*Jan Sanders*	Understanding Woodturning	*Ann & Bob Phillips*
Decorative Techniques for Woodturners	*Hilary Bowen*	Useful Woodturning Projects	*GMC Publications*
Faceplate Turning: Features, Projects, Practice	*GMC Publications*	Woodturning: A Foundation Course	*Keith Rowley*
Green Woodwork	*Mike Abbott*	Woodturning Jewellery	*Hilary Bowen*
Illustrated Woodturning Techniques	*John Hunnex*	Woodturning Masterclass	*Tony Boase*
Keith Rowley's Woodturning Projects	*Keith Rowley*	Woodturning: A Source Book of Shapes	*John Hunnex*
Make Money from Woodturning	*Ann & Bob Phillips*	Woodturning Techniques	*GMC Publications*
Multi-Centre Woodturning	*Ray Hopper*	Woodturning Wizardry	*David Springett*
Pleasure & Profit from Woodturning	*Reg Sherwin*		

WOODCARVING

The Art of the Woodcarver	*GMC Publications*	Understanding Woodcarving	*GMC Publications*
Carving Birds & Beasts	*GMC Publications*	Wildfowl Carving Volume 1	*Jim Pearce*
Carving Realistic Birds	*David Tippey*	Wildfowl Carving Volume 2	*Jim Pearce*
Carving on Turning	*Chris Pye*	The Woodcarvers	*GMC Publications*
Decorative Woodcarving	*Jeremy Williams*	Woodcarving: A Complete Course	*Ron Butterfield*
Essential Woodcarving Techniques	*Dick Onians*	Woodcarving for Beginners: Projects, Techniques & Tools	
Lettercarving in Wood	*Chris Pye*		*GMC Publications*
Practical Tips for Turners & Carvers	*GMC Publications*	Woodcarving Tools, Materials & Equipment	*Chris Pye*

PLANS, PROJECTS, TOOLS & THE WORKSHOP

The Incredible Router	*Jeremy Broun*	Sharpening Pocket Reference Book	*Jim Kingshott*
Making & Modifying Woodworking Tools	*Jim Kingshott*	The Workshop	*Jim Kingshott*
Sharpening: The Complete Guide	*Jim Kingshott*		

TOYS & MINIATURES

Designing & Making Wooden Toys	*Terry Kelly*	Making Wooden Toys & Games	*Jeff & Jennie Loader*
Fun to Make Wooden Toys & Games	*Jeff & Jennie Loader*	Miniature Needlepoint Carpets	*Janet Granger*
Making Board, Peg & Dice Games	*Jeff & Jennie Loader*	Turning Miniatures in Wood	*John Sainsbury*
Making Little Boxes from Wood	*John Bennett*	Turning Wooden Toys	*Terry Lawrence*

CREATIVE CRAFTS

Celtic Knotwork Designs	*Sheila Sturrock*	Embroidery Tips & Hints	*Harold Hayes*
Collage from Seeds, Leaves and Flowers	*Joan Carver*	Making Knitwear Fit	*Pat Ashforth & Steve Plummer*
The Complete Pyrography	*Stephen Poole*	Miniature Needlepoint Carpets	*Janet Granger*
Creating Knitwear Designs	*Pat Ashforth & Steve Plummer*	Tatting Collage	*Lindsay Rogers*
Cross Stitch on Colour	*Sheena Rogers*		

UPHOLSTERY AND FURNITURE

Care & Repair	*GMC Publications*	Making Shaker Furniture	*Barry Jackson*
Complete Woodfinishing	*Ian Hosker*	Pine Furniture Projects	*Dave Mackenzie*
Furniture Projects	*Rod Wales*	Seat Weaving (Practical Crafts)	*Ricky Holdstock*
Furniture Restoration (Practical Crafts)	*Kevin Jan Bonner*	Upholsterer's Pocket Reference Book	*David James*
Furniture Restoration & Repair for Beginners	*Kevin Jan Bonner*	Upholstery: A Complete Course	*David James*
Green Woodwork	*Mike Abbott*	Upholstery: Techniques & Projects	*David James*
Making Fine Furniture	*Tom Darby*	Woodfinishing Handbook (Practical Crafts)	*Ian Hosker*

DOLLS' HOUSES AND DOLLS' HOUSE FURNITURE

Architecture for Dolls' Houses	*Joyce Percival*	Making Period Dolls' House Furniture	*Derek & Sheila Rowbottom*
A Beginners' Guide to the Dolls' House Hobby	*Jean Nisbett*	Making Victorian Dolls' House Furniture	*Patricia King*
The Complete Dolls' House Book	*Jean Nisbett*	Miniature Needlepoint Carpets	*Janet Granger*
Easy-to-Make Dolls' House Accessories	*Andrea Barham*	The Secrets of the Dolls' House Makers	*Jean Nisbett*
Make Your Own Dolls' House Furniture	*Maurice Harper*		
Making Dolls' House Furniture	*Patricia King*		
Making Period Dolls' House Accessories	*Andrea Barham*		

OTHER BOOKS

Guide to Marketing	*GMC Publications*	Woodworkers' Career & Educational Source Book	*GMC Publications*

VIDEOS

Carving a Figure: The Female Form	*Ray Gonzalez*	Woodturning: A Foundation Course	*Keith Rowley*
The Traditional Upholstery Workshop		Elliptical Turning	*David Springett*
Part 1: *Drop-in & Pinstuffed Seats*	*David James*	Woodturning Wizardry	*David Springett*
The Traditional Upholstery Workshop		Turning Between Centres: The Basics	*Dennis White*
Part 2: *Stuffover Upholstery*	*David James*	Turning Bowls	*Dennis White*
Hollow Turning	*John Jordan*	Boxes, Goblets & Screw Threads	*Dennis White*
Bowl Turning	*John Jordan*	Novelties & Projects	*Dennis White*
Sharpening Turning & Carving Tools	*Jim Kingshott*	Classic Profiles	*Dennis White*
Sharpening the Professional Way	*Jim Kingshott*	Twists & Advanced Turning	*Dennis White*

MAGAZINES

WOODTURNING • WOODCARVING • TOYMAKING
FURNITURE & CABINETMAKING • BUSINESSMATTERS
CREATIVE IDEAS FOR THE HOME

The above represents a full list of all titles currently published or scheduled to be published. All
are available direct from the Publishers or through bookshops, newsagents and specialist retailers.
To place an order, or to obtain a complete catalogue, contact:

GMC Publications, 166 High Street, Lewes, East Sussex BN7 1XU United Kingdom
Tel: 01273 488005 Fax: 01273 478606

Orders by credit card are accepted